CHRIST PRESENT IN FAITH

CHRIST PRESENT IN FAITH
Luther's View of Justification

Tuomo Mannermaa

Edited and Introduced by
Kirsi Stjerna

Fortress Press
Minneapolis

CHRIST PRESENT IN FAITH
Luther's View of Justification

First Fortress Press edition 2005

Translated from the German "In ipsa fide Christus adest: Der Schnittpunkt zwischen lutherischer und orthodoxer Theologie," originally published in Tuomo Mannermaa, *Der im Glauben gegenwärtige Christus: Rechtfertigung und Vergottung. Zum ökumenischen Dialog* (Hannover: Lutherisches Verlagshaus, 1989).

Cover image: ©Stefano Bianchetti/CORBIS
Cover design: Kevin van der Leek Design Inc.
Book design: James Korsmo

Mannermaa, Tuomo.
  [In ipsa fide Christus adest. English]
  Christ present in faith : Luther's view of justification / Tuomo Mannermaa ; edited and introduced by Kirsi Stjerna.
      p. cm.
  Includes bibliographical references and index.
  ISBN 0-8006-3711-9 (alk. paper)
  1. Luther, Martin, 1483-1546. 2. Justification (Christian theology)—History of doctrine—16th century. I. Stjerna, Kirsi Irmeli, 1963- II. Title.
  BR333.5.J8M3613 2005
  234'.7'092—dc22

                                                          2004027587

The paper used in this publication meets the minimum requirements of American National Standard for Information Sciences — Permanence of Paper for Printed Library Materials, ANSI Z329.48-1984.

Manufactured in the U.S.A.

09   08   07   06   05   2   3   4   5   6   7   8   9   10

Contents

Editor's Foreword

One of the truly Archimidean insights of the European Reformation was into how human beings can become reconciled to God in Christ. Martin Luther's notion of justification, as it is called, marked a crucial turning point in Christian theology and sparked momentous changes in all of Christianity. Yet what precisely did Luther mean by justification? How does it take place? And how are humans, who remain sinners, affected, and their salvation effected, by justification? Tuomo Mannermaa, a premier historical theologian from Finland, has opened these vital questions again in a new, exciting, and increasingly influential way through his work on Martin Luther's writings. This volume makes available for the first time in English Mannermaa's single most important work on the subject. Originally published in Finnish twenty-five years ago, it appeared as *In ipsa fide Christus adest: Luterilaisen ja ortodoksisen kristinuskonkäsityksen leikkauspiste* [In faith itself Christ is really present: The point of intersection between Lutheran and Orthodox theology]. It was published again in 1981, in an unaltered format. A few years later the book was translated into German by Hans-Christian Daniel and Juhani Forsberg—"In ipsa fide Christus adest: Der Schnittpunkt zwischen lutherischer und orthodoxer Theologie"—and published in Tuomo Mannermaa, *Der im Glauben gegenwärtige Christus: Rechtfertigung und Vergottung. Zum ökumenischen Dialog* (Hannover: Lutherisches Verlagshaus, 1989). This edition is based on the German text.

It has stimulated new interest and reinvigorated struggle with the classic Christian texts, including Luther's. Needless to say, Professor Mannermaa is pleased to see his work being offered now in English to an international audience.

Regarding texts quoted in the study and their translation, whenever possible the English Luther quotations are from the American Edition of *Luther's Works* (*LW*). Where no reference to *LW* is given, the translation is our own, due to the absence of the text or passage concerned in the American Edition. The Bible quotations are taken from the New Revised Standard Version (NRSV), with the exception of the biblical verses in *LW* quotations, which have been left untouched. In terms of inclusive language issues, as an editor I have suggested alternative readings in brackets to correct the unintended linguistic exclusivity that is sometimes an issue with the English and German expressions used in the text. The reader should note that Finnish pronouns do not specify gender, and thus the Finnish text is naturally inclusive in this regard, whether in reference to humans (the word *hän* means both "she" and "he") or to God. It is hoped that the alternative words offered in brackets bring out the intended inclusivity of the content of the book and that clarity is not compromised in the process.

Some of the concepts employed in the Finnish text did not translate easily into English. Mannermaa is well aware of the "weight" that comes with certain philosophically loaded terms such as "ontological," "essential," "real," "substantial," etc. In this work, he frequently uses the Finnish word *onttinen*, which could be translated directly as "ontic." In the editing process, and in consultation with Mannermaa himself, the word has been translated "ontological," which is the word Mannermaa prefers to use in his current writing. Readers should note that the study will not address the different nuances between the terms "ontic" and "ontological," and no arguments are made in this regard. The word "ontological," in Mannermaa's use, underscores the reality of things and events.

While most of the translation is as literal as possible, in the editing process some changes were made to state better in English the original meaning. No changes were made in regard to content, however. If any mistakes were made in this process, I take full responsibility and offer my apologies.

A select bibliography is included at the end of the book, and offers a representative selection of Mannermaa's academic works. It focuses on treatises written for academic conversation; a number of Mannermaa's articles and books have not been noted. Studies by other authors are also listed, representing the best of "Finnish Luther research."

As the bibliography shows, not much is available as yet from Mannermaa or his colleagues for an English-speaking audience. An important introduction to this topic and school of thought remains the book edited by Carl E. Braaten and Robert W. Jenson, *Union with Christ: The New Finnish Interpretation of Luther* (Eerdmans, 1998). That volume contains articles by both Mannermaa and his students and colleagues, with comments from American scholars. Also important is *Caritas dei: Beiträge zum Verständnis Luthers und der gegenwärtigen Ökumene* (ed. Oswald Bayer, Robert W. Jenson, Simo Knuuttila; Luther-Agricola-Gesellschaft, 1997), a Festschrift in honor of Mannermaa's sixtieth birthday, with a number of significant articles relating to issues close to Mannermaa's heart and research interests. That book also includes an extensive chronological bibliography of Mannermaa's works from 1961 to 1997.

We hope to see more of Mannermaa's works published in English in the future. One book to be translated is his *Pieni kirja Jumalasta* (A small book on God) (Jyväskylä, 1995), in which Mannermaa offers a lively, heartfelt theology of central issues related to God and the human being's relationship to God. It presents insights soundly rooted in a lifelong dialogue with Luther, shaped by the wisdom that comes both from a life fully lived and from extensive study, and presented in a language that speaks to the hearts and minds of people today, across language and cultural barriers.

I am honored to assist in the production of this translation. As a student of Mannermaa since the 1980s, I join the many students and colleagues of his who are indebted to his intelligent teaching and creative thinking, and his passionate pursuit of Luther's theology—something that is contagious and can lead one into a lifelong love affair with Luther.

I would like to offer thanks to the many people behind this project: I wish to thank first of all Dr. Mannermaa for this remarkable book and for his review of the translation. Many thanks go to his longtime friend and colleague Dr. Juhani Forsberg—a major contributor to the production of this edition and co-translator of the earlier German edition—for working with the text and logistics and for his overall support of Mannermaa's work through the decades. Warmest thanks to Mrs. Inkeri Mannermaa, who "got online" before her husband did and served as intermediary between the different parties collaborating on this project. Thanks also go to Dr. Risto Saarinen for sharing his bibliographical information and his excellent Luther-studies website. In the editing process, consultation on the English and on theological concepts was graciously offered by Dr. Eric Crump and Dr. Brooks Schramm, my colleagues at the Lutheran Theological Seminary at Gettysburg, where Mannermaa's works are much appreciated.

The Institute for Luther Studies at the Lutheran Theological Seminary at Gettysburg is a "silent" sponsor of this book: Mannermaa's thesis has been discussed in the institute's annual Luther Colloquy on several occasions, and Mannermaa has thus joined the voices heard there, even if he has not been able to join us "in the flesh." With this publication, Mannermaa will continue to speak to and teach the Luther Colloquy participants, and the larger audience beyond, in the years to come.

Last but not least, a thank you to Fortress Press for its foresight in publishing this work. Many thanks to Michael West for his interest in publishing Mannermaa's works and to James Korsmo for his editorial work.

Editor's Introduction

"The Mannermaa school," "the Finnish Luther research"—these have become internationally known terms among scholars as well as clergy and laity interested in Martin Luther. In North America, conversation has been going on for a decade on the findings and arguments of one of the most original Luther scholars in recent memory.

Tuomo Mannermaa's name is already enshrined in the annals of Luther scholarship. No respected research, in any language, on Luther's central theology—especially around his views on justification, faith, and love—can afford not to refer to or comment on Mannermaa's substantial work from the last forty years. It is indeed appropriate to speak of the "Mannermaa school," as his position has become established among a growing group of scholars who have tested and supported his original thesis and continued his work with a number of dissertations and articles.[1] Mannermaa's work continues a long tradition of strong Luther research in Finland, shaped in the early twentieth century by the then professors of systematic theology at the University of Helsinki, Lennart Pinomaa and Lauri Haikola. Since the 1980s, significant, groundbreaking Luther research has been conducted in their footsteps in the department of systematic theology under Professor Mannermaa's leadership.

The controversial nature of Mannermaa's thesis has to do with his effectiveness in unfolding the fullness and radicality of Luther's theology of justification. The radical nature of Mannermaa's thesis, as with Luther's theology itself, has to do most of all with "reality talk." That is, how do we, and how does Luther, talk about what "really" happens for and to and in believers in the act of justification and in relation to the Divine? Is it a matter of more than "just words" and belief? Controversial also is Mannermaa's suggestion that some of the earlier Luther interpretations may have been wrong or at least blind in this regard.

The traditional emphasis in Lutheran interpretation—both in preaching and in teaching the gospel the Lutheran way—has been that in the act of justification believers are declared righteous through "imputation" of righteousness and thus considered guilt-free before God. Instead of joining this chorus, Mannermaa points out in Luther's theology a heretofore neglected emphasis on the real, reality-altering presence of God that occurs along with the act of imputation, in which the believer is made righteous and thus one with God. In other words, in his interpretation of Luther's language, Mannermaa maintains that Luther gives equal emphasis to both the "forensic" and the "effective" sides of righteousness, to how justification means both being declared forgiven before God and being made holy in a personal union with God. Mannermaa's work shows how the language of imputation and forensic justification cannot do justice to the entirety of Luther's theology of justification (or reveal his potential as a spiritual teacher). He demonstrates that, for Luther, justification has real effects; that Christ the Redeemer does not operate only for us but also in us. The depth of Luther's theology of justification by faith cannot be appreciated fully without coming to appropriate conclusions about what it means in reality when Christ comes to live in us and makes us one with God—and thus, in a sense, gods. Needless to say, such a statement in Lutheran circles is prone to cause a stir.

If Mannermaa's attention to what is traditionally called the "effective side of righteousness" is already controversial, even more so is his suggestion, or rather thesis, that the idea of divinization, *theosis*, is a central part of Luther's theology and particularly of the doctrine of justification.

Mannermaa argues for this concisely and convincingly, drawing his evidence from Luther himself. Mannermaa states that the concept of participation in God (*theosis*) is inherent in all of Luther's theology. And indeed, Luther speaks frequently about "God's indwelling" or "inhabitation" in the human being (e.g., WA 4:280, 2-5; WA 3:106, 14-15). The focus in Luther is not on what a human becomes but on what is done "to" the human being and what this means to the human being in relation to God: deification is about participation in God, the focus being on God's act.[2]

Mannermaa points out that for Luther "*theosis* is based causally on the divinity of God." It comes to the believer, initiated by God, through a "nihilization" that destroys one's constant effort to make oneself god and to justify oneself.[3] For Luther, divinization has to do with God's own way of being the loving God who comes to the world in the Word: "God is in *relation* to himself in the movement of the Word (*Deum Patrem sibi suum apud se verbum proferre*) at the same time that he *is* this movement of the Word. This understanding of the being of God is the basis for understanding the being-present-of-Christ in faith."[4] A beautiful quote from Luther used by Mannermaa says it well: "Thus the righteousness of Christ becomes our righteousness through faith in Christ, and everything that is his, even he himself, becomes ours ... and he who believes in Christ clings to Christ and is one with Christ and has the same righteousness with him."[5] This idea of participation is, according to Mannermaa, the key to understanding different topics in Luther's theology.

Using the language of divinization and union with God and talking about a new reality that comes with justification, Luther's theology sounds mystical and essentially in tune with both the Orthodox and Roman Catholic views on what happens to human beings in their grace-initiated, faith-based relationship with God in Christ. It is precisely these expressions about union with Christ and participation in the divine life that have not found their way as yet into the vocabulary of Lutherans in general, whose traditional "Lutheran language" has been limited in this regard. At the same time, these very same expressions and ideas first of all excite conversation partners from other traditions where this kind of "ontological" language is not unfamiliar and, second, show the breadth of Luther's spirituality.[6] In modern conversation about spirituality and particularly Lutheran spirituality, the contribution of Mannermaa and other Finns is foundational. As Scott Hendrix states, "Finnish scholarship has performed a service by calling attention again to the new reality in Christ which constituted the heart of Luther's spirituality."[7]

Mannermaa's work calls for a critical rereading of all Luther's works and a rethinking of the foundations of Lutheran theology and the tradition of Luther interpretation. This work is important not only to Luther scholars seeking the most authentic reading of Luther, but also for Lutherans in general in affirming their own theological and spiritual identity in an ecumenical context.

Actually, Mannermaa's thesis and questions make every Luther scholar wonder if he or she has read Luther correctly—or been too much shaped by the Lutheran confessional tradition and perhaps missed the "authentic Luther." Depending on how one answers that question, one is either with Mannermaa, not yet convinced, or perhaps simply opposed to his position.

The excitement around Mannermaa's research is still somewhat new on the North American continent, while in Europe his work is already being followed by a second phase of research in dialogue with his initial findings. In 1993 Mannermaa visited North America, lecturing at the meeting of the International Luther Congress that was held at Luther Seminary, St. Paul, Minnesota. There he and a group of Finnish colleagues and students presented his radical readings of Luther. Three years later, in 1996, he visited St. Olaf College in Minnesota, leading a seminar on Luther and sharing the views of the Finns with the one hundred or so participants. Both events stimulated quite a conversation, and it is still going on. As a result of these meetings there was a great demand for Mannermaa's ideas to be made available in English. In 1998, professors Carl E. Braaten and Robert W. Jenson edited the work *Union with Christ: The New Finnish Interpretation of Luther* (Eerdmans, 1998), which contains articles by both Mannermaa and his closest circle of students, with comments from American scholars, and is still the only book-length introduction to the Finnish Luther research that evolved around Mannermaa.

As characterized in the introduction to that book, the "Mannermaa school is revising a century of Luther interpretation dominated by German Protestant theologians, who notoriously read Luther under the spell of neo-Kantian presuppositions. This is true of a long line of German Luther scholarship from Albrecht Ritschl to Gerhard Ebeling."[8] Through his fresh reading of Luther with an intentional effort to put preexisting assumptions and categories aside, Mannermaa indeed came to challenge a whole range of Protestant, predominantly German, Luther scholarship. He names particularly Karl Holl and his school, including Heinrich Bornkamm, Emanuel Hirsch, Hans Rückert, Erich Seeberg, and Erich Vogelsang as representatives of the (in his view) erroneous interpretation of Luther that started from wrong philosophical premises.[9]

What Mannermaa criticizes the most in Holl and his school is their too quick and unnecessary rejection of everything "ontological" in Luther ["ontological," to put it simply, referring to "being" and the "real"]. Mannermaa has challenged their rejection of the idea of ontological participation with his reading of Luther's central idea that "in faith itself Christ is really present," with the emphasis being on the words "really present." Arguing from Luther's Christology, which draws from the teachings of the early church and patristic theology, Mannermaa shows exactly how "ontological" it is for Luther that Christ is in and for us—really, truly, and personally. From this christological starting point, Luther can talk about righteousness as a human being becoming one with God through a real exchange of attributes between the sinner and Christ. Mannermaa posits that ontological language is exactly the language needed to present what Luther is actually saying, whether it is about God's presence in the believer, Christ's *communicatio idiomatum* in the act of justification, or about the effect of the sacraments. Reading Luther in his medieval context and not trying to make him stand in opposition to the mystical tradition, Mannermaa reveals the ontological dimension of Luther's theology and thereby Luther's mystical and realistic view of the personal union between the believer and God. Based on Mannermaa's reading, this is vintage Luther, this is genuine Luther—and, as we can see, this is a surprisingly ecumenical Luther who stands tall as a spiritual teacher today.[10]

Mannermaa's perspective contributes significantly to the ecumenical dialogues between Lutherans and other denominations by introducing a Luther whose theology has many more bridges with the older Christian theologies and spiritualities than the previously predominant Luther interpretation. Mannermaa in a sense puts Luther's own texts against the interpretative history and finds that the "real Luther" is much more powerful than the one there presented.

Before introducing the book at hand, let me briefly describe Professor Mannermaa's career and research journey. Tuomo Mannermaa, born in 1937, earned his Candidacy of Theology (equivalent to Master of Theology) in 1964 and later his doctorate in theology in 1970, both at the University of Helsinki, Finland. He served as an assistant professor in the department of systematic theology at the University of Helsinki from 1976 to 1980, and as a professor of ecumenics from 1980 to 2000, after which he retired. He was awarded an honorary doctorate by the University of Copenhagen in 2000.

His dissertation, *Lumen fidei et obiectum fidei . . . Die Spontaneität und Rezeptivität der Glaubenserkenntnis im frühen Denken Karl Rahners* (1970), examined the use of Karl Rahner's transcendental method in philosophy and theology. This work led him to investigate the relationship between theology and philosophy in patristic, scholastic, and modern (post-Kantian) Roman Catholic theology. In 1972 the Archbishop of Finland, Martti Simojoki, appealed to Mannermaa to report on the history of the Leuenberg Concord (the council of European Reformed churches) and their fundamental method for unity. This assignment gave Mannermaa an insight into German Protestant theology and church politics in that context. This research resulted in a book, *Von Preussen nach Leuenberg: Hintergrund und Entwicklung der theologischen Methode in der Leuenberger Konkordie* (Hamburg, 1981). The Evangelical Lutheran Church and the Russian Orthodox Church had already started regular meetings in the early 1970s. In 1973 Archbishop Simojoki invited Mannermaa to join the Finnish delegation and again appealed to him to look for a starting point and a reasonable foundation for the ensuing negotiations. In 1977, in Kiev, Mannermaa presented his argument that such a starting point and connection from the Lutheran side can be found in the Lutheran teaching on Christ present in faith (*in ipsa fide Christus adest*). This doctrine, Mannermaa argued, is analogous to the Orthodox doctrine of *theosis*. Furthermore, he argued, Luther is familiar with the *theosis* doctrine and it is present in his theology in many ways. The presentation on justification and deification given in Kiev was published the same year in the Finnish theological periodical *Theologinen Aikakauskirja* (6 [1977]) and stimulated much interest. Because of the general interest in his presentation and the topic, Mannermaa then expanded the article into a longer study on the subject, the result of which is this book, now translated into English.

Even if the initial impulse for the new Finnish Luther research came from the context of concrete ecumenical conversations between churches, very soon the new Luther study became established as a purely "scientific" theological enterprise, funded substantially by the Finnish Academy (Suomen Akatemia). Several dissertations have been written as a result of this original project and some are still awaiting publication.[11]

Mannermaa himself has been a prolific writer, in addition to mentoring numerous works of others. Always engaged in firsthand research, Mannermaa has written a number of books as well as many articles and has participated in public conversation on pertinent issues of church and society in Finland. With his heart in ecumenical work, and always willing to offer his expertise to benefit the ecumenical conversation, he has personally and through his books contributed significantly to the European ecumenical scene. His works have been applauded and embraced by both professional theologians as well as ministers and laity of the church. Many of his works have become textbooks and shaped the thinking of numerous students. His works have provided both intellectual challenge and spiritual nourishment, and have significantly assisted the work toward the unity of Christian churches.

This book, *In ipsa fide Christus adest*, in its previous versions in Finnish and German has had a continuing and diligent audience; it has shaped many budding theologians as required reading in the study of systematic and ecumenical theology at the theological department at the University of Helsinki. — still in existence

In this book Mannermaa carefully analyzes Luther's *Lectures on Galatians*. These lectures were not printed at the time Luther gave them, but later a commentary was published based on the notes taken by the students. Mannermaa, aware of this fact, uses primarily Luther's extant lecture notes (included in WA), and only when the text there is too fragmentary does he consult and quote the published text—always making sure that the line of thought in the published text corresponds with that of Luther's lecture notes. He also draws from his study on Luther's theology of love, *Kaksi rakkautta: Johdatus Lutherin uskonmaailmaan* (Two kinds of love: Introduction to Luther's world of faith [Juva, 1983]), a work that also became a standard textbook in Helsinki. Mannermaa in these works aims to provide a Luther study that is sensitive and applicable to ecumenical issues—especially in the dialogue between the Finnish Lutheran and the Russian Orthodox Church—while yet considering the study as an independent work with a specific focus. With an eye on the ecumenical conversation and the use of the book as a textbook, Mannermaa chooses to include abundant, direct Luther quotations with translations. This allows the reader to read with Mannermaa, straight from Luther, and to follow Mannermaa's interpretation firsthand. As the study relates directly to scholarship on the "normative doctrine," as Mannermaa calls it, he explicitly wants to retain authentically Lutheran terminology.

This treatise, relatively short in length but massive in content, lifts up Luther's central tenets and arguments about faith, justification, love, and Christian life. Mannermaa systematically explains Luther's view of faith and love; of sin and human life; of the work and nature and gifts of Christ; of the reality of justification; of the Christian life, struggle, and love; of the role of the church and sacraments in the work of God's Word; and the holiness as well as the reality of sin that characterizes the life of those one with Christ—and all this around the idea of *theosis*. The book serves as a detailed introduction to Luther's theology and reveals its special nuances, and in that process efficiently familiarizes the reader with Luther's basic terminology.

The work argues for and centers on Luther's radical insight about justification being a godly act of divinization that changes a person's relationship with God ontologically. Arguing in light of the Orthodox teaching of *theosis*, Mannermaa proves through systematic reading of Luther that the idea of divinization, which happens because of Christ and in faith, is at the heart of Luther's theology. Not only offering an occasion for ecumenical mutual understanding of the basics of Christian faith, it dramatically shifts the central emphasis in Lutheran theology and thus spirituality. As said before, this perspective changes the emphasis from talk about "declared" righteousness and forgiveness to talk about "made righteous" and holy, emphasizing not only Christ as a "favor" but also as a "gift," and with all this, portraying Christian life in faith as a new reality with real effects and transformation—thus with more responsibilities in the world for those divinized with Christ's presence. This notion of Christ's incarnation and redemption leading into real participation of the divine in human life has implications not only in terms of theological emphasis but also in terms of how Lutherans can experience life in faith and speak about it.

With his articulate and insightful works, Mannermaa will continue to participate in the ever-expanding conversation on the basics and future of Lutheran spirituality. His interpretation highlights Luther's flexibility as a spiritual teacher beyond denominational boundaries by lifting up Luther's central theological principles and letting them speak in their own language.

Abbreviations

EA   *Dr. Martin Luthers sämmtliche Werke*, 67 vols. (Erlangen: Heyder & Zimmer, 1826–1857)

LW   *Luther's Works*. American Edition. 55 vols., ed. Jaroslav Pelikan and Helmut Lehmann. (Philadelphia and St. Louis: Fortress and Concordia, 1955–1986)

NRSV   *The Holy Bible*. New Revised Standard Version. (New York & Oxford: Oxford University Press, 1989)

WA   *D. Martin Luthers Werke*. Kritische Gesamtausgabe, 60 vols. (Weimar: Herman Böhlaus Nachfolger, 1883–1980)

WA,DB   *D. Martin Luthers Werke*. Kritische Gesamtausgabe. *Die Deutsche Bibel*, 12 vols. (Weimar, 1906–1961)

CHRIST PRESENT IN FAITH

Introduction

Late-nineteenth and early-twentieth-century Protestant scholarship has considered it difficult, if not impossible, to find a mutual point of contact between the Orthodox and the Lutheran understandings of Christian faith. Particularly the patristic-Orthodox "doctrine of divinization" and the Lutheran "doctrine of justification" have been considered mutually contradictory.

It is important not to blur the differences between the Orthodox and Lutheran theologies, as both have their own complexities. However, one needs to notice that the presumption that has dominated Protestant scholarship and has considered the doctrines of divinization and justification as in sharp contrast to each other is based on certain premises that have emerged in the course of the history of modern theology. I would like to mention here two of these premises: first of all, the influence of Kant and neo-Kantianism, which has resulted in the view that the relationship of a human being with God should be seen as an "ethical relation"; secondly, the influence of kerygmatic theology, affected by the understanding of kerygma in dialectical theology.

These and some other positions have led to a situation in which it has been difficult to do justice to those texts of Luther in which his terminology actually borders on expressions characteristic of mysticism when discussing the union between God (Christ) and the believer.[1] At the same time, it has also been a widely held view that the Orthodox doctrine of divinization is based on a "physical" way of thinking that displaces the "personalistic" form of thought.[2]

From its own standpoint, apart from these Protestant assumptions, the core of the Orthodox doctrine of divinization can be described as follows: The divine life has been revealed in Christ. In the communion of the church, which is the body of Christ, human beings become participants in this divine life. In this way, they become partakers of the "divine nature" (2 Peter 1:4). This "nature," that is, this divine life, permeates their essence like leaven, restoring it to its original state.[3]

Thus, the concept of participation in the divine life in Christ is at the core of the doctrine of divinization. In patristic thinking, the idea of divinization was often expressed through concepts that were taken from Greek ontology. This does not mean, however, that the doctrine itself could be labeled entirely Hellenistic, as was suggested by the Ritschlian school. This Ritschlian thesis relied, in essence, on a philosophical premise according to which the "physical" relationship with God, based on the union of "being," must be categorically kept apart from the "personal-ethical" relation to God. In patristic thinking itself, however, the "ethical" and the "ontological" were not separated in this modern fashion. Thus, the doctrine of divinization rests on the presupposition that the human being can actually participate in the fullness of life in God. It is precisely this participation that is called "divinization" (or "deification"; Greek, *theosis, theopoiesis*; Latin, *deificatio*) in the tradition of the early church and in the Orthodox church—a term which has often been misunderstood by Protestants.

Without pursuing the question whether the technical term "divinization" can genuinely and appropriately express the whole of the patristic and Orthodox doctrine of salvation, in this work the term is used to express the more or less established view of salvation of the early church from which the christological dogma developed. The doctrine of divinization is expressed most classically in the theology of Athanasius.

I am aware of the fact that "divinization" is not the only basic term to sum up and characterize the understanding of Christian faith as represented by Athanasius. Jaroslav Pelikan, for example, understands *theosis* as "transformation." An interesting critique of this view, in turn, has been presented by Dietrich Ritschl. For Pelikan, the central principle of the theology of Athanasius is the symbol of light. For this reason, Ritschl suggests, in a study on Athanasius dedicated to the Russian theologian Vitaly Borovoy,[4] that it would have been more consistent of Pelikan to use the word "transfiguration" for divinization. This suggestion is of significance because in 1977, in the Finnish-Russian theological discussions held in Kiev, the same Vitaly Borovoy presented an interpretation of the entirety of the Orthodox doctrine of salvation, using "transfiguration" as the key concept. Thus, at least in their starting points, both transfiguration and divinization point to the same theology of Athanasius. (It is not possible, however, for this study to solve the special issues of Athanasius research. Rather, references will be made to the above-mentioned work of Dietrich Ritschl, which also provides the reader with the history of Athanasius scholarship.) In this study I will be using the term "divinization" as an already established term in the history of dogma, while remaining aware of the problems related to this choice.

A more precise or detailed presentation of the Orthodox doctrine is not part of the objective of this work. No actual comparisons between the Orthodox and the Lutheran concepts of faith will be made, either. Instead, the aim of this study is to look for a theological motif in the Lutheran concept of Christian faith which would be analogous to the notion of divinization and could thus serve as a point of contact with Orthodox theology.

This particular aim has its roots in a series of theological discussions between the Evangelical Lutheran Church of Finland and the Russian Orthodox Church. In these discussions, the partners have dedicated themselves to unraveling the knots in their mutual relations and searching for an appropriate starting point for this process. Instead of setting church-political goals, these churches have struggled to find a mutual theological point of contact that would be as solid as possible and provide the partners with a basis on which to conduct future discussions.

When one looks for the motifs in Lutheran theology analogous to the concept of divinization, one's attention is drawn to the fact that Lutheran theology and tradition is undoubtedly familiar with the notion of God's essential indwelling in the believer (*inhabitatio Dei*). The classic quotation on this *inhabitatio* is found in the *Formula of Concord* (FC), which is one of the Lutheran confessional texts (1577). According to this passage, God, in the very fullness of God's essence, is present in those who believe in God.

It is important to recognize that the text explicitly rejects notions that God in godself would not "dwell" in Christians and that only God's "gifts" would be present in them.[5] However, from the point of view of Lutheran self-understanding, the FC gives rise to a problem, namely, that the FC's definition concerning the relation between "justification" and "divine indwelling" is different from that found in Luther's theology, at least as far as terminology is concerned. Thus, in the FC, "justification by faith" merely denotes the forgiveness of sins that is "imputed" to Christians on the basis of the perfect obedience and complete merit of Christ. At the same time, the *inhabitatio Dei* is made a separate phenomenon, logically *subsequent* to justification. This classic excerpt reads as follows:

> We must also explain correctly the discussion concerning the indwelling of God's essential righteousness in us. On the one hand, it is true indeed that God the Father, Son, and Holy Spirit, who is the eternal and essential righteousness, dwells by faith in the elect who have been justified through Christ and reconciled with God, since all Christians are temples of God the Father, Son, and Holy Spirit, who impels them to do rightly. But, on the other hand, this indwelling of God is not the righteousness of faith of which St. Paul speaks and which he calls the righteousness of God, on account of which we are declared just before God. This indwelling follows the preceding righteousness of faith, which is precisely the forgiveness of sins and the gracious acceptance of poor sinners on account of the obedience and merit of Christ.[6]

In its argument that the presence of the Trinity in faith is not the same phenomenon as the "righteousness of faith," the FC draws on the later theology of Melanchthon, on which much of Lutheran theology after Luther has relied. In the theology of the FC, justification is understood in a one-sidedly forensic manner, that is, only as a reception of the forgiveness that is "imputed" to Christians for the sake of the obedience and merit of Christ. The *inhabitatio Dei* is considered a *consequence* of this "righteousness of faith," i.e., the forgiveness of sins.

In the theology of Luther, however, the relation between justification and the divine indwelling in the believer is defined differently. Luther's notion of the "righteousness of faith" is permeated by christological thinking. He does not separate the person (*persona*) of Christ and his work (*officium*) from each other. Instead, *Christ himself*, both his person and his work, *is* the Christian righteousness, that is, the "righteousness of faith." Christ—and therefore also *his entire person and work*—is really and truly present in the faith itself (*in ipsa fide Christus adest*). The favor (*favor*) of God (i.e., the forgiveness of sins and the removal of God's wrath) and his "gift" (*donum;* God himself, present in the fullness of his essence) unite in the person of Christ. At least on the level of terminology, justification and the real presence of God in faith are in danger of being separated by the one-sidedly forensic doctrine of justification adopted by the FC and most of subsequent Lutheranism. In Luther's theology, however, both these motifs are completely united in the person of Christ. Christ is both the *favor* and the *donum*, without separation or confusion (in other words, neither is separate or to be confused with the other), to use the Chalcedonian expressions. According to Luther, Christ (both his person and his work), who is present in faith, *is* identical with the righteousness of faith. Thus, the notion that Christ is present in the Christian occupies a much more central place in the theology of Luther than in the Lutheran theologies that came after him. Thus, it is easier to find a point of contact with the patristic concept of divinization in Luther's theology than in later Lutheran theologies. The idea of the divine life in Christ that is present in faith lies at the very center of the theology of the Reformer.

This discrepancy between the view of the FC and the position of Luther makes one wonder which view actually represents "the Lutheran" understanding of this doctrine. I would argue that, even though the FC is part of the normative confessional texts accepted by many Lutheran churches, with regard to this *locus* the Lutheran teaching is most fully expressed particularly in the doctrine of justification formulated by Luther himself. In fact, this argument is based on the interpretation presented in the FC itself. At the end of the FC's article on justification (Article III), an explicit reference is made to Luther's commentary on the Epistle to the Galatians (1535).[7] The FC says that this "beautiful and splendid exposition" (i.e., Luther's commentary) contains the "proper explanation" (*"eigentliche Erklärung"*) of the righteousness of faith. Moreover, the Latin text urges everyone to "consult" the commentary and to "read it diligently."[8] Because the FC itself says that Luther's *Lectures on Galatians* has the final authority concerning the doctrine of justification, it is possible to present the Lutheran understanding of this issue on the basis of this commentary of Luther. Luther himself did not have his *Lectures on Galatians* printed, but the commentary was edited on the basis of lecture notes taken by listeners. When I was writing this study, I therefore compared the published text of the *Lectures* with Luther's extant shorthand notes. In those cases where the language of the original notes was too fragmentary, I took the quotations from the printed text—each time making sure, however, that the line of thought in the published text corresponded with the content of the notes.[9]

There is an additional reason why it is justifiable to state that the Lutheran doctrine of justification should draw on the theology of Luther himself: he, too—and not only the representatives of Lutheran Orthodoxy and Pietism—is one of the important "spiritual teachers" of the Lutheran church worldwide. (His books have been popular and of central importance among the Finnish Lutherans, for instance.) Luther's teachings continue to be important for the current life of the church and spirituality, as well as for today's theology.

From the point of view of scholarly interest, it is readily apparent that the theology of Luther constitutes the historical starting point for the development of Lutheran doctrine. In the history of Lutheran theology, with each issue, Luther himself always seems to be "the other" focus of discussion. Whether the issues involve the relations between Luther and Melanchthon, Luther and the Lutheran confessions, Luther and Lutheran orthodoxy, Luther and Pietism, or Luther and modern neo-Protestantism, these relationships can properly be appropriated only when Luther's own theology is first examined. As long as Luther scholarship produces reliable results in this area, a firm foundation can be established for future discussions concerning the views of later Lutheranism and in relation to the doctrines of the Orthodox church.

To my knowledge, the doctrine of divinization and that of justification have never been brought into real confrontation with each other. After I had read a paper on the topic at Kiev, I noticed, however, that Regin Prenter points out that divinization and justification are interrelated. Having stated that in faith the believer's being is taken into God's being, which is love, Prenter says in a footnote: "In my opinion, this insight finds expression in a doctrine which stands on a patristic basis, namely, the Orthodox doctrine of the human being's divinization. This doctrine, on which suspicion has so often been cast by the Protestant side, gives expression to the same intention as does the evangelical doctrine of justification by faith alone: only through God himself, that is, through the Holy Spirit, can a human being believe in God, and love God, and thus be justified. God in Christ is himself the human being's righteousness before God. This implies that the human being who is righteous in faith is taken into the being of God."[10] Georg Kretschmar also points out the fact that Luther often says that in faith a human being becomes "God."[11]

These views presented by Prenter and Kretschmar are not incidental, nor are they only individual views of certain scholars, but rather express the conclusions to be drawn from the mainstream of Luther research carried out since Karl Holl. Holl's school—the significant representatives of which include scholars such as Heinrich Bornkamm, Emanuel Hirsch, Hanns Rückert, Erich Seeberg, and Erich Vogelsang[12]—paid special attention to Luther's doctrine of justification. It was because of the influence of this school that the one-sidedly forensic interpretation turned out to be characteristic of the Lutheranism subsequent to Luther. Even if the roots of Luther's views in the Christology of the early church were not the primary object of interest for Holl, Hirsch, and Vogelsang, their research on Luther's concept of faith brought up inevitably the essential interrelatedness of Christology and the theology of faith in Luther's thinking. On this basis, many scholars (for example, Wilhelm Maurer and Lauri Haikola) have pointed out that Luther agrees with the fundamental principles embraced by the Christology of the early church. Thus, in his programmatic treatise "Die Einheit der Theologie Luthers,"[13] Maurer interprets the entire theology of the Reformer from the standpoint of an Athanasian type of Christology, which Luther then accentuates in his own way. The close interrelatedness of Luther's doctrine of justification and the Christology of the early church serves as the fundamental starting point for this study.

The first part (I) of this study shows that Luther's doctrine of justification rests on the christological thinking of the early church, which he interprets in a particular way (ch. 1). In his human nature, according to Luther, Christ *really* bears the sins of all human beings; in his divine nature, he is eternal righteousness and life. Christ wins the battle between sin and righteousness, and this takes place within his own person. Faith, in turn, means participation in the person of Christ. When a human being is united with God, he or she becomes a participant not only in the human but also in the divine nature of Christ. At the same time, a kind of "communication of attributes" occurs: the attributes of the essence of God—such as righteousness, life, power, etc.—are communicated to the Christian. In all this, Christ in his person is both God's "favor" and God's "gift" at the same time.

From Luther's point of view, the *fides charitate formata* position of scholasticism signifies only a partial "divinization" (ch. 2). According to the Reformer, Christ himself—not love—is the form (i.e., "the ontological reality," *Seinswirklichkeit*) of faith.[14] Thus, God is present in faith in the very fullness of God's essence. Faith, in turn, justifies precisely because it "takes hold of and possesses" the present Christ. Luther's understanding of the law leads to a similar interpretation of the relationship between faith and Christ: the spiritual function of the law is to lead human beings into union with Christ (ch. 3). Christ and the Christian are made one person (ch. 4). Owing to this, the Reformer states frequently that in faith the human being becomes "God" (ch. 5).

The second part (II) focuses on the notion of the present Christ being the key to Luther's understanding of the relationship between faith and sanctification. Christ, whose presence and efficaciousness in faith are real, is the primary subject and the actual agent of the good works of the believer (ch. 6). This idea is the very core of the frequently used parable of a tree and its fruit.

The key to Luther's understanding of the relationship between the real and the "declared" (imputated) righteousness of the Christian can be found in the concept of *in ipsa fide Christus adest*. Luther often says that faith is the "beginning" of real righteousness, and imputation "perfects" it (ch. 7). The Reformer's doctrine of the believer as simultaneously righteous and a sinner can also be understood from this point of view.

Luther's interpretation of the Christian's struggle in faith[15] is based on his view of Christians as partly righteous and partly sinners. In the battle between the "flesh" and the "Spirit," the principle of the fight is the Spirit of Christ, whose presence is real and ontological (ch. 8). The continuity of the life of a Christian in faith rests on the fact that the Spirit of Christ, who is present in a Christian as a kind of "other subject," "intercedes" for him or her by "sighing" incessantly to God (ch. 9). A human being cannot discern the "cry" of the Spirit through sense experience, and therefore the Spirit seeks to encourage those in distress to take hold of the "word" (*solum verbum habemus*).

Luther's notion of the believer's ontological and real participation in God in Christ becomes apparent in the striking physical-natural imagery with which Luther portrays the means of grace: the word is the "womb," the church is the "mother," and the ministry of the word is the "father." They give birth and shape to the Christian (ch. 10). All this takes place because of the efficaciousness of the means of grace, which is objective: Christians do not act themselves but are objects of action; they do not give birth but are born (ch. 11). However, the objectivity of the means of grace does *not* imply the inability of these means to convey Christ, whose presence in faith is real: *Sic ut Christus sit obiectum fidei, imo non obiectum, sed, ut ita dicam, in ipsa fide Christus adest.* (Christ is the object of faith, or rather not the object but, so to speak, the One who is present in the faith itself.)

Part I

THE DOCTRINE OF JUSTIFICATION AND CHRISTOLOGY

Chapter 1

The Basis for Justifying Faith

Christ as the "greatest sinner" (*maximus peccator*)

Luther's concept of Christian faith is based on the christological thinking of the early church, which he, however, accentuates in a specific manner. In Luther's view, the doctrine of incarnation, a dogma shared by the entire early church, is most closely connected with that of justification. The second person of the Trinity—the Logos, who is born in eternity—"did not regard it as something to be exploited" (Phil. 2:6) to be in the form of God (*in forma dei*) but, out of sheer love, took the form of a slave (*forma servi*) by becoming a human being. According to Luther, however, the Logos did not take upon himself merely human nature, in a "neutral" form, but precisely the concrete and actual human nature. This means that Christ *really* has and bears the sins of all human beings in the human nature he has assumed. Christ is the greatest sinner (*maximus peccator, peccator peccatorum*). The Reformer says:

> And all the prophets saw this, that Christ was to become the greatest thief, murderer, adulterer, robber, desecrator, blasphemer, etc., there has ever been anywhere in the world. He is not acting in His own Person now. Now He is not the Son of God, born of the Virgin. But He is a sinner, who has and bears the sin of Paul, the former blasphemer, persecutor, and assaulter; of Peter, who denied Christ; of David, who was an adulterer and a murderer, and who caused the Gentiles to blaspheme the name of the Lord (Rom. 2:24). In short, He has and bears all the sins of all [people] in His body—not in the sense that He has committed them but in the sense that He took these sins, committed by us, upon His own body, in order to make satisfaction for them with His own blood.[1]

The text of Luther's lecture notes continues in words that are not found in the published text, making apparent the realistic way in which Luther thinks of Christ's union with sinners. The Logos communicates himself to the human nature of "thieves and sinners"; moreover, he is even "immersed" in it.

> And so He is regarded as someone who is among thieves—even though He is innocent Himself, and even more so, because of His own free will and by the will of the Father He wanted to communicate Himself to the body and blood of those who were thieves and sinners. Therefore He is immersed in all.[2]

Thus, the special emphasis of Luther's theology of incarnation lies precisely in the notion that Christ was, in the human nature which he assumed, the greatest sinner of all. The Reformer is aware of the oddity of this thought and therefore frequently defends his view.

> "But it is highly absurd and insulting to call the Son of God a sinner and a curse!" If you want to deny that He is a sinner and a curse, then deny also that He suffered, was crucified, and died. For it is no less absurd to say, as our Creed confesses and prays, that the Son of God was crucified and underwent the torments of sin and death than it is to say that He is a sinner or a curse. But if it is not absurd to confess and believe that Christ was crucified among thieves, then it is not absurd to say as well that He was a curse and a sinner of sinners. . . . Is. 53:6 speaks the same way about Christ. It says: "God has laid on Him the iniquity of us all." These words must not be diluted but must be left in their precise and serious sense. For God is not joking in the words of the prophet; He is speaking seriously and out of great love, namely, that this Lamb of God, Christ, should bear the iniquity of us all. But what does it mean to "bear"? The sophists reply: "To be punished." Good. But why is Christ punished? Is it not because He has sin and bears sin? That Christ has sin is the testimony of the Holy Spirit in the Psalms. Thus in Ps. 40:12 we read: "My iniquities have overtaken Me"; in Ps. 41:4: "I said: 'O Lord, be gracious to Me; heal Me, for I

have sinned against Thee!'"; and in Ps. 69:5: "O God, Thou knowest My folly; the wrongs I have done are not hidden from Thee." In these psalms the Holy Spirit is speaking in the Person of Christ and testifying in clear words that He has sinned or has sins. These testimonies of the psalms are not the words of an innocent one; they are the words of the suffering Christ, who undertook to bear the person of all sinners and therefore was made guilty of the sins of the entire world.[3]

Christ as the "greatest person" (*maxima persona*) and the "only sinner" (*solus peccator*)

Luther's concept of Christ as the "greatest sinner" discloses a premise which is of essential importance for his theology of incarnation and doctrine of atonement. According to this premise, Christ is a kind of "collective person," or, as the Reformer formulates it himself, the "greatest person" (*maxima persona*), in whom the persons of all human beings are really united. Christ *is* every sinner:

> This is the most joyous of all doctrines and the one that contains the most comfort. It teaches that we have the indescribable and inestimable mercy and love of God. When the merciful Father saw that we were being oppressed through the Law, that we were being held under a curse, and that we could not be liberated from it by anything, He sent His Son into the world, heaped all the sins of all [people] upon Him, and said to Him: "Be Peter the denier; Paul the persecutor, blasphemer, and assaulter; David the adulterer; the sinner who ate the apple in paradise; the thief on the cross." In short, be the person of all men, the one who has committed the sins of all men.[4]

This idea of Christ as the "greatest person" (*maxima persona*) culminates in the notion of Christ as the "only sinner" (*solus peccator*). After the Logos has become flesh, there is no sin at all anywhere else but in his person. Christ is immersed (*submersus*) in all sins, and all sins are immersed in him. This idea is the starting point for Luther's doctrine of atonement. Without going into details, I shall present here briefly the aim of this doctrine, which has not yet been studied sufficiently.

As a human being, Christ is the "greatest sinner of all"; at the same time, as the Logos, he is God, the "perfect righteousness and life." Therefore his person is marked by an extreme tension and a most profound contradiction. By his divine nature Christ is the "Divine Power, Righteousness, Blessing, Grace, and Life."[5] These divine attributes fight against sin, death, and curse—which also culminate in his person—and overcome them. Hence, there is no sin or death or curse any more because "all sin is gathered together" in Christ and he was thus the "only sinner."

It is important to appreciate that the conquest of the forces of sin and destruction takes place within Christ's own *person*. He won the battle between righteousness and sin "in himself" (*triumphans in seipso*). Sin, death, and curse are first conquered in the person of Christ, and "thereafter" the whole of creation is to be transformed through his person. Salvation is participation in the person of Christ.[6]

Faith as participation in the person of Christ

It is a central idea of Luther's theology that in faith human beings *really* participate in the person of Christ, and in the divine life and victory that come with him. Or, to say it the other way round: Christ gives his person to us through faith. "Faith" means participation in Christ, in whom there is no sin, death, or curse.

> To the extent that Christ rules by His grace in the hearts of the faithful, there is no sin or death or curse. But where Christ is not known, there these things remain. And so all who do not believe lack this blessing and this victory. "For this" as John says, "is our victory, faith."[7]

In Luther's view, faith is a victory precisely because it unites the believer with the person of Christ, who, in himself, *is* the victory.

According to the Reformer, justifying faith does not merely signify a reception of the forgiveness imputed to a human being for the sake of the merit of Christ, which is the aspect emphasized by the *Formula of Concord*. Faith as real participation in Christ means participation in the institution of "blessing, righteousness, and life" which has taken place in Christ. Christ himself *is* life, righteousness, and blessing, because God is all this "by nature and in substance" (*naturaliter et substantialiter*).[8] Therefore, justifying faith means participation in God's essence in Christ.

The core of Luther's concept of participation finds expression in the notion of "happy exchange," according to which Christ takes upon himself the sinful person of a human being and bestows his own righteous person upon him or her. What takes place here between Christ and the believer is a kind of communication of attributes: Christ, the divine righteousness, truth, peace, joy, love, power, and life, gives himself to the Christian. At the same time, Christ "absorbs" the believer's sin, death, and curse into himself.[9] As Christians thus *really* participate in Christ, they have no sin or death anymore. In Luther's view, scholastic theology can be characterized as teaching precisely the opposite to this: according to the scholastics, sin is a quality attached to the substance, human nature. The "true theology," in contrast, teaches that "there is no longer any sin in the world" because all sin "is gathered together in Christ" who has conquered it within his own person. Wherever a human being is united with Christ in faith, there sin is truly devoured. Luther says:

> Now that Christ reigns, there is in fact no more sin, death, or curse—this we confess every day in the Apostles' Creed when we say: "I believe in the holy church." This is plainly nothing else than if we were to say: "I believe that there is no sin and no death in the church. For believers in Christ are not sinners and are not sentenced to death but are altogether holy and righteous, lords over sin and death who live eternally." But it is faith alone that discerns this, because we say: "I believe in the holy church." If you consult your reason and your eyes, you will judge differently. For in devout people you will see many things that offend you; you will see them fall now and again, see them sin, or be weak in faith, or be troubled by a bad temper, envy, or other evil emotions. "Therefore the church is not holy." I deny the conclusion that you draw. If I look at my own person or at that of my neighbor, the church

will never be holy. But if I look at Christ, who is the Propitiator and Cleanser of the church, then it is completely holy; for He bore the sins of the entire world.

Therefore where sins are noticed and felt, there they really are not present. For, according to the theology of Paul there is no more sin, no more death, and no more curse in the world, but only in Christ, who is the Lamb of God that takes away the sins of the world, and who became a curse in order to set us free from the curse. On the other hand, according to philosophy and reason, sin, death, etc., are not present anywhere except in the world, in the flesh, and in sinners. For the theology of the sophists is unable to consider sin any other way except metaphysically, that is: "A quality clings to a substance or a subject. Therefore just as color clings to a wall, so sin clings to the world, to the flesh, or to the conscience. Therefore it must be washed away by some opposing motivations, namely, by love." But the true theology teaches that there is no more sin in the world, because Christ, on whom, according to Is. 53:6, the Father has laid the sins of the entire world, has conquered, destroyed, and killed it in His own body. Having died to sin once, He has truly been raised from the dead and will not die anymore (Rom. 6:9). Therefore wherever there is faith in Christ, there sin has in fact been abolished, put to death, and buried. But where there is no faith in Christ, there sin remains.[10]

Because to Luther faith denotes a real union with the person of Christ, his understanding of faith is directly anchored in Christology. Christ and faith belong together "essentially." Against this background it is readily understandable that Luther agrees with the Christology of the early church, according to which the divine nature of Christ is of the same essence as God (the Father). Luther's criticism of Arius is thus immediately based on the idea of justifying faith. The line of thought is as follows: God is "by nature and in substance" (*naturaliter et substantialiter*) righteousness, blessing, and life.[11] Christ can conquer sin, death, and curse in himself only if he *is* righteousness, blessing, and life in himself—that is, if he is God in essence. Having said that the believer, being united with Christ, has no sin, death, or curse anymore, Luther continues by combining the doctrine of the divinity of Christ with that of justification by faith:

These are the chief doctrines of our theology, which the sophists have obscured. Here you see how necessary this article of faith is: Christ is the Son of God. When Arius denied this, it was necessary for him to lose the article of redemption as well. For the "overcoming of sin in Himself" belongs together with the fact that Christ is a human being. Thus He must be true God as well. Namely, the divine power must be there so that the Law, death, and wrath could be destroyed, and divinity is needed so that He can give life in Himself. It is characteristic of the divine majesty to annihilate and to create. Therefore Scripture says that Christ destroyed death and sin in Himself and granted life. Therefore, whoever begins to deny the divinity of Christ will lose the whole of Christianity and becomes a Turk. This is why I have told you so often that the article of justification must be learned well. As long as we teach that we are justified through Christ, we have to show that Christ is the true Son of God. These are our speculations which are not useless but work powerfully against the righteousness of human works.[12]

Hence, because faith means a real union with Christ, and because in Christ the Logos is of the same essence as God the Father, therefore the believer's participation in the essence of God is also real. This is what Luther means when he speaks of Christ as a "gift." Christ is not only the favor (*favor*) of God, that is, forgiveness, but also, in a real manner, a "gift" (*donum*).

Christ as a "gift" (*donum*)

The idea that Christ is both God's favor (*favor*) and God's gift (*donum*) permeates the entire theology of Luther. "Favor" signifies God's forgiveness and the removal of his wrath. In other words, "favor" is the attitude toward the human being in the "subject" of God. Christ as a "gift," in turn, denotes the real self-giving of God to the human being. The presence of Christ in faith is real, and he is present in it with all his essential attributes, such as righteousness, blessing, life, power, peace, and so forth. Thus, the notion of Christ as a "gift" means that the believing subject becomes a participant in the "divine nature." Indeed, the Reformer often refers to the same passage in the Second Letter of Peter on which also the patristic doctrine of *theopoiesis* is based.[13]

Luther develops the idea of Christ as a gift especially in his well-known piece of writing called *Against Latomus*. Besides, even though he does not thematically discuss the distinction between "gift" and "favor" in his *Lectures on Galatians*, the distinction itself, as well as the concept of the "gift," is manifest throughout the commentary. Thus, the notion of Christ as a gift, as well as the Reformer's "realistic" interpretation of the relationship between faith and Christ, both emerge in the following quote where he states that the Christian is "greater than heaven and earth" because the gift in the Christian's heart, Christ, is greater than heaven and earth:

> Therefore a Christian, properly defined, is free of all laws and is subject to nothing, internally or externally. But I purposely said, "to the extent that he is a Christian" (not "to the extent that he is a man or a woman"); that is, to the extent that he has his conscience trained, adorned, and enriched by this faith, this great and inestimable treasure, or, as Paul calls it, "this inexpressible gift" (2 Cor. 9:15), which cannot be exalted and praised enough, since it makes [people] sons [and daughters] and heirs of God. Thus a Christian is greater than the entire world. For in [one's] heart [one] has this seemingly small gift; yet the smallness of this gift and treasure, which [one] holds in faith, is greater than heaven and earth, because Christ, who is this gift, is greater.[14]

The text reveals how realistically Luther thinks of the presence of the "gift," that is, Christ. His *Lectures on Galatians* include many other similar passages. In the following extract, which is taken from a sermon in the so-called *Church Postil*, Luther expresses his thoughts concerning "favor," "gift," and "participation in the divine nature" with particular clarity:

> This is one of those apposite, beautiful, and (as St. Peter says in 2 Pet. 1) precious and very great promises given to us, poor miserable sinners: that we are to become participants in the divine nature and be exalted so highly in nobility that we are not only to become loved by God through Christ, and have His favor and

grace as the highest and most precious shrine, but also to have Him, the Lord Himself, dwelling in us in His fullness. Namely (he wants to say), His love is not to be limited only to the removal of His wrath from upon us, and to having the fatherly heart which is merciful to us, but we are also to enjoy this love (otherwise it would be wasted and lost love, as it is said: "to love and not to enjoy . . ."), and gain great benefit and riches from it.[15]

Thus, in addition to being the "favor" (forgiveness), Christ is also the "gift." In other words, the presence of Christ means that the believer participates in forgiveness of sins and in the "divine nature." And when participating in God's essence, the Christian also becomes a partaker of the attributes of this essence.

Faith and the communication of attributes (*communicatio idiomatum*)

The notion that Christians are partakers of the "divine nature" means that they are "filled with all the fullness of God." God's righteousness makes Christians righteous; God's "life lives in them"; God's love makes them love, and so forth. Luther calls this event by various names, one of which is "happy exchange." As regards the content of this event, however, the most accurate expression might be the "communication of attributes" (*communicatio idiomatum*), which the Reformer admittedly uses less frequently but which expresses the underlying idea well. This communication is not to be identified with the christological *communicatio idiomatum*, but it must be understood in an analogical way. The idea of the communication of attributes as well as its relationship with the notion of *inhabitatio Christi* is presented clearly, for example, in the following quote:

And so we are filled with "all the fullness of God." This phrase, which follows a Hebrew manner of speaking, means that we are filled in all the ways in which He fills [a person]. We are filled with God, and He pours into us all His gifts and grace and fills us with His Spirit, who makes us courageous. He enlightens us with His light, His life lives in us, His beatitude makes us blessed, and His love causes love to arise in us. Put briefly, He fills us in order that everything that He is and everything He can do might be in us in all its fullness, and work powerfully.[16]

Faith communicates the divine attributes to the human being, because Christ himself, who is a divine person, is present in faith. Therefore, the believer is given all the "goods" (*bona*) of God in faith. It is easy to see that in Luther's theology the concept of justifying faith and the idea of the indwelling of Christ in faith cannot be separated, as we have already preliminarily stated. Justification does not merely denote the imputation of Christ's merit to the sinner, which would then be followed by the *inhabitatio Dei* as a separate phenomenon. In Luther's theology, justification in the meaning of the FC and the communication of attributes are both expressions and different sides of one and the same event. Especially in connection with the doctrine of the communication of attributes, this can be seen very clearly. It is precisely the Christ present in justifying faith who communicates God's saving attributes to the believer in the "happy exchange." God *is* righteousness, and in faith the human being participates in righteousness; God *is* joy, and in faith the human being participates in joy; God *is* life, and in faith the human being participates in life; God *is* power, and in faith the human being participates in power, and so forth.

The notion of the believer's real participation in the "divine nature" in Christ, and the doctrine of the communication of attributes related to it, reveals how essentially and inseparably the Reformer's theology of faith is based on the Christology of the early church and its emphasis on the real and ontological communication of attributes and the twofold nature of Christ. In Luther's theology, however, the patristic concept of redemption with its notion of *theopoiesis* is interpreted with the help of the doctrine of justification. Consequently, the distinctiveness of Luther's theology of faith becomes evident in the context of Luther's criticism of the scholastic doctrine of salvation. The scholastic view was summarized in the formula "*fides charitate formata*" (faith formed by love). The Reformer replaces this with his own position, which can be freely expressed as "*fides Christo formata*" (faith formed by Christ).

Chapter 2

Faith Formed by Christ

The *"fides charitate formata"* position criticized by Luther

The intellect—love

As mentioned earlier, Luther holds that participation in the divine life in Christ takes place in faith. In order to analyze the Reformer's concept of faith, it is helpful to examine his criticism of scholastic interpretations of faith, which were familiar to him.[1]

According to the scholastic notion which Luther criticizes particularly sharply, faith means that something which is beyond the reach of rational knowledge is regarded as truth; thus, in this view, faith belongs to the domain of the intellect but is logically uncertain.

The relationship with God can be realized, however, with the help of the human being's basic tendency (*tendentia*)—namely, the will, or the *e-motio*, that is, love. The view generally held in scholasticism maintains that love is an inclination to an object. In a sense, it is a "blind" movement (or motion, to use the more philosophical term) toward the object. Most essentially, love is a movement toward the transcendent and infinite Being, namely, God. If this motion is graced (*gratia infusa*) and thus receives the powers of grace, it "reaches" the Triune God and "rises" to God.

Central to the concept described above is that the human being is brought into true fellowship with God by *love*, which is elevated by grace. Consequently, faith as such is considered insufficient as the center, or organon, of the human being's relationship with God. It is admitted that faith gives the human being information about the possible objects of love, but it is regarded as "dead" and "lifeless" without love elevated and inspired by grace.

Faith as matter (materia) *and love as form* (forma)
In the scholastic theology criticized by Luther, the relationship
between faith and love was defined through metaphysical concepts.
According to the scholastic definition, faith is seen as the material
cause (*materia*, matter), whereas love is the formal cause (*forma*,
form). Love inspired by grace is the *forma*, that is, the divine reality
(*göttliche Seinswirklichkeit*) that gives faith its form, or "(in-)forms" it.
Because love thus gives faith reality, faith changes from dead knowing
into living, active, and—as it was also called—"colorful" knowing.
All in all, this understanding of justification can be crystallized in
one slogan: faith formed by love (*fides charitate formata*), that is,
faith is brought into the divine reality by love. With the help of this
infused love, the human being's love changes from a corrupt love for
the worldly to love for God. In this way, human beings can find the
right order of love, and perform works that are free from corrupt
love for the worldly and are in accordance with love of God; and by
these works they can be saved, that is, reach God.

Love as the "substance" and grace as an "accident"
Luther criticizes very sharply the scholastic conception of faith. He
focuses his criticism on the incorrect definition of the relationship
between faith and love in the *fides charitate formata* position. It is
important to notice that the reason for the Reformer's criticism
of the scholastic view (described above) is not, in the first place,
the fact that grace is understood as an actual reality (*forma*) that
is intimately connected with the Christian's essence. Luther, too,
maintains that the righteousness which is present in faith—that is,
Christ—*is* within the Christian as an actual reality. Furthermore,
Luther also calls the righteousness of faith a "formal righteousness"
(*formalis iustitia*), that is, a real righteousness that is there in the
reality of the Christian's being.[2] The Reformer's criticism of the
scholastic doctrine is directed against the notion that the proper
reality of salvation is love. This is the focus of Luther's criticism:
even if elevated and divinized by grace, the human being's love
nevertheless still remains substantially human love.

This criticism presented by the Reformer means that he
does not accept the notion included in the scholastic solution
that regards grace as a *habitus* or an "accident" attached to the

human being's substance, that is, as an inherent quality (*qualitas inhaerens*).[3] If grace is merely an "accident" giving the "substance" (i.e., the human love which exists in itself) a new quality, then the permanent and fundamental element constituting the human being's relationship with God is his or her own love. In that case, as mentioned above, grace is merely an inherent quality attached to the substance, the human being's love. The very point of Luther's theology of faith is directed against this view. Grace is not—as one could say in this context—an "accident," but its nature is precisely that of a "substance." To rephrase, grace is God in Christ. This reality has its being in itself—not in or from something else. While it is true that the Christ present in faith is the real righteousness that is in the reality of the Christian's being, at the same time, this righteousness retains its "substantial" (being in itself) character. To rephrase once again, the *formalis iustitia* is Christ himself,[4] and even when this righteousness is present in a human being, it remains what it is with respect to essence—namely, it remains God's *own* righteousness, of which the human being cannot boast. Even Christ *in nobis* is Christ *extra nos*.

The nature of grace as "a reality which exists in itself" finds expression in the thought repeated often by Luther that faith is a "living," "mighty," and "active" thing (*Ding*) that does not lie "idle" in the soul like a "color" does "on an object." The idea behind these characteristic images can be expressed by saying that, from the point of view of the Reformer, grace is not an "accidental" (being in another) but a "substantial" (being in itself) reality. Grace is Christ himself.

Love as the law
There is also another central aspect included in Luther's above-mentioned criticism of the scholastic doctrine of grace. The Reformer states that if love, as elevated by grace and as a natural tendency towards God, is regarded as the constitutive center, or organon, of salvation, then the human being's relationship with God must be thought of, as a whole, within the framework of the law.[5] As human reality, love remains—even as elevated—a human striving, the human being's movement toward God. Therefore, it belongs to the domain of the law.

Love as the way to salvation must be excluded, because in the "before God" (*coram Deo*) perspective Christ is the only righteousness of human beings.

"*Fides Christo formata*"

Christ as the form of faith (Christus forma fidei)
Luther's criticism of the scholastic teaching of salvation can be summarized as follows: In a human being, righteousness is "alien righteousness"—even though in faith this alien reality *really* determines the believer's being, which it is intimately connected with (*formalis iustitia*). What is "alien" here is not the elevated human love, but Christ himself and his real presence.

This criticism of the *fides charitate formata* position, which also expresses the core of Luther's Reformation program, can be formulated by saying that the form of faith is not love but Christ himself. Luther does, indeed, use the slogan *Christus forma fidei*.[6] From Luther's standpoint, the difference between the scholastic teaching and Luther's view can be phrased as follows: the former teaches *fides charitate formata*, whereas the Reformer teaches *fides Christo formata*.[7] To Luther, faith has the actual divine reality (*Seinswirklichkeit*), that is, *forma*. This faith, *forma*, is Christ himself present in faith, the only way of salvation.

"*Therefore faith justifies because it takes hold of and possesses this treasure, the present Christ*"
Luther's notion of faith cannot be understood correctly if Christ is regarded merely as an object of faith in the same way as any item can be an object of human knowledge. Rather, the object of faith is a person who is present, and therefore he is, in fact, also the "subject." Luther says that Christ is the object of faith, but not merely the object; rather, "Christ is present in the faith itself" (*in ipsa fide Christus adest*). Faith is knowledge that "sees nothing." Thus, according to the Reformer's description, faith is like the cloud in the Most Holy Place of the Temple of the Old Covenant in which God wanted to dwell. (Cf. 1 Kings 8:12: "Then Solomon said, 'The Lord has said that he would dwell in thick darkness.'")

It is in the darkness of faith that Christ sits on his throne in all his reality and reigns, just as God did in the darkness and cloud in the Most Holy Place of the Temple. In the following quotation, which is a passage central to Luther's theology of faith, the Reformer crystallizes his idea of *Christus forma fidei:*

> But we substitute that love for faith. And while they say that faith is the "monogram," mere initial letters, but love is its living colors and completion, we say in opposition that faith takes hold of Christ and that He is the form that adorns and informs faith as color does the wall. Therefore Christian faith is not an idle quality or an empty husk in the heart, which may exist in a state of mortal sin until love comes along to make it alive. But if it is true faith, it is a sure trust and firm acceptance in the heart, which takes hold of Christ. Christ is namely the object of faith, or rather not the object but, so to speak, the One who is present in the faith itself. Thus faith is a sort of knowledge or darkness that nothing can see. Yet the Christ of whom faith takes hold is sitting in this darkness as God sat in the midst of darkness on Sinai and in the temple. Therefore our actual "formal righteousness" is not a love that informs faith; but it is faith itself, a cloud in our hearts, that is, trust in a thing we do not see, in Christ, who is present although He cannot be seen at all.
>
> Therefore faith justifies because it takes hold of and possesses this treasure, the present Christ. But how He is present—this is beyond our thought; for there is darkness, as I have said. Where the confidence of the heart is present, therefore, there Christ is present, in that very cloud and faith. This is the actual, formal righteousness on account of which a man is justified; it is not on account of love, as the sophists say. In short, just as the sophists say that love forms and fulfills faith, so we say that it is Christ who forms and fulfills faith or who is the form [*actus; Seinswirklichkeit*] of faith. Therefore the Christ who is grasped by faith and who lives in the heart is the true Christian righteousness, on account of which God counts us righteous and grants us eternal life. Here there is no work of the Law, no love; but there is an entirely different kind of righteousness, a new world above and beyond the Law. For Christ or faith is neither the Law nor the work of the Law.[8]

This passage shows what the Reformer means by his well-known expression according to which Christ is the actual mystery of faith. Moreover, it is obvious that because Christ himself is present in faith, faith cannot be any "supposition" which could lie "idle or still" in the soul. Lifeless, dead, and empty faith is an "absolute" faith, that is, a faith detached from Christ.[9] What makes this kind of faith alive, however, is not love inspired by grace but the present Christ. He brings along the attributes of the essence of God, such as righteousness, power, life, and freedom—in short, "life and blessedness" (Large Catechism).

The idea of Christ present in faith is also the key to the well-known and often quoted passage in Luther's *Preface to Romans* where he discusses the theology of faith:

> Faith, however, is a divine work in us which changes us and makes us to be born anew of God, John 1[:12-13]. It kills the old Adam and makes us altogether different men, in heart and spirit and mind and powers; and it brings with it the Holy Spirit. O it is a living, busy, active, mighty thing, this faith. It is impossible for it not to be doing good works incessantly.[10]

The idea presented above about the presence of Christ in faith as real not only reveals the inner integrity of Luther's theology of faith but also makes understandable the Reformer's criticism of the, in his view, erroneous interpretation of divinization.

"Christus praesentissimus in nobis": A criticism of the erroneous interpretation of divinization

The premise of the erroneous interpretation of divinization is that Christ is not really present "down" in the faith but that he is "up" in heaven. This interpretation maintains that human beings' relationship with God is based on a striving love, in which they move toward transcendence, that is, toward Christ "up" in heaven. According to Luther, however, fellowship with Christ based on this type of love is always *partial*; it is an incessant and unceasing movement toward transcendence, and it always remains in the domain of the "works of a beggar." By contrast, the Reformer emphasizes that God has come "down" in the very fullness of God's essence, that is, God has become a human being. Whoever has faith is already now really "in heaven," because all the fullness of God is in Christ, and because the presence of Christ is real. Luther says:

> This is the true faith of Christ and in Christ, through which we become members of His body, of His flesh and of His bones (Eph. 5:30). Therefore in Him we live and move and have our being (Acts 17:28). Hence the speculation of the sectarians is vain when they imagine that Christ is present in us "spiritually," that is, speculatively, but is present really in heaven. Christ and faith must be completely joined. We must simply dwell in heaven; and Christ must be, live, and work in us. But He lives and works in us, not speculatively but really, most presently and most effectively.[11]

The criticism that Luther presents here is directed primarily against the so-called Spiritualists of the Reformation era, but the same criticism applies to scholastic theology as well. As mentioned several times already, the core of the view criticized by Luther is the understanding of faith as a kind of accident, or an inherent quality that clings to the heart apart from Christ. Christ is in heaven, which the human being therefore tries to reach with the help of love elevated by the Holy Spirit. In his typical manner, Luther says the following about this idea of *fides charitate formata*, which, according to him, is characteristic of both the Spiritualists and scholastic theology:

> The fanatical spirits today speak about faith in Christ in the manner of the sophists. They imagine that faith is a quality that clings to the heart apart from Christ. This is a dangerous error. Christ should be set forth in such a way that apart from Him you see nothing at all and that you believe that nothing is nearer and closer to you than He. For He is not sitting idle in heaven but is completely present with us, active and living in us as chapter two says (2:20): "It is no longer I who live, but Christ who lives in me," and here: "You have put on Christ."[12]

According to Luther, faith is the right way of becoming a partaker of God because it possesses the whole fullness of the essence of God in Christ. It is in justifying faith that participation in the "divine life" takes place. Therefore, we must take Luther's notion of the law into account when we analyze his concept of faith. His interpretation of the essence and function of the law also leads to the idea of Christian sharing in the "divine life."

Chapter 3

The Law and Participation in the "Divine Life"

The law belongs in the "world"

The total inability of the law to act as a way to salvation
A central aspect of Luther's christologically-based idea of faith is his notion of the law, which also serves as a kind of antagonistic and contrapuntal theme in his theology of faith.

The first point Luther makes about law is his absolute denial of the law's capability to serve as a way to salvation. This means that works of love must not be required of human beings with the intention that they should achieve righteousness through such works. To regard love as the basis for one's salvation would be the primary source of corruption of faith. Contrary to this, God wants, out of pure and sheer love, to grant God's forgiving righteousness—that is, Godself—to human beings and to be their "life and blessedness." The law cannot create this kind of "strong and powerful" life, nor does it make a human being a new creation. Only faith, that is, Christ alone, can give birth to a new human being. "Hypocrites," that is, those who want to become righteous through works, trouble themselves day and night, but "unskillfully," because "the law is not a source of either advice or refuge." Efforts to achieve salvation and find peace of conscience with the help of the law—that is, through works demanded by the law—are works of "Sisyphus" and "the daughters of Danaus." A hypocrite is "milking a billy goat" and "holding a sieve." Luther says:

> Anyone who wanted to grow rhetorical here could develop these words further: actively, passively, and neutrally. Actively: the Law is a weak and beggarly element because it makes men weaker and more beggarly. Passively: because it does not have of itself the power and ability to grant or confer righteousness.

31

And neutrally: of itself it is weakness and poverty, which afflict and trouble the weak and the poor more and more all the time. Trying to be justified through the Law, therefore, is as though someone who is already weak and sick were to ask for some even greater trouble that would kill him completely but meanwhile were to say that he intends to cure his disease by this very means; or as though someone suffering from epilepsy were to catch the plague in addition; or as though a leper were to come to another leper, or a beggar to another beggar, with the aim of giving him assistance and making him rich. As the proverb says, one of these is milking a billy goat and the other is holding the sieve![1]

The hazardous and weakening effect of the law

Luther uses many different and strong expressions when describing the "Sisyphus character" of the "righteousness of the law." For example:

> Trying to be justified by the Law is like counting money out of an empty purse, eating and drinking from an empty dish and cup, looking for strength and riches where there is nothing but weakness and poverty, laying a burden upon someone who is already oppressed to the point of collapse, trying to spend a hundred gold pieces and not having even a pittance, taking clothing away from a naked man, imposing even greater weakness and poverty upon someone who is sick and needy, etc.[2]

Luther's criticism of the law as a way of salvation has overtones that resemble the criticism of the human weakness presented by the new era's "mature human being" (though from a totally different standpoint). The righteousness of the law makes human beings weak and powerless. Luther, however, does not envision an *Übermensch* but a human being who is strong in the power of God's grace:

> Therefore everyone who falls away from the promise to the Law, from faith to works, is doing nothing but imposing an unbearable yoke upon himself in his weak and beggarly condition (Acts 15:10). By doing this he becomes ten times as weak and beggarly, until he finally despairs, unless Christ comes and sets him free.

The same thing is shown by the Gospel story (Mark 5:25-26) about the woman who had suffered from a flow of blood for twelve years and had suffered much under many physicians, on whom she had spent all that she had; but she could not be cured by them but grew worse with longer care. Therefore those who perform the works of the Law with the intention of being justified through them not only do not become righteous but become twice as unrighteous; that is, as I have said, through the Law they become weaker, more beggarly, and incapable of any good work. I have experienced this both in myself and in many others. Under the papacy I saw many of the monks who performed many great works with burning zeal in order to acquire righteousness and salvation; and yet there was nobody in the world more impatient, weaker, and more miserable than they, and nothing more unbelieving, fearful, and desperate than they. Political officials, who were involved in the most important and difficult issues, were not as impatient and as womanishly weak, or as superstitious, unbelieving, and fearful as such self-righteous men.[3]

The Reformer says that those who "wish to be justified and made alive" within the framework of the order of the law

fall further short of righteousness and life than do tax collectors, sinners, and harlots. These latter cannot rest on confidence in their own works, which are such that they cannot trust that they will obtain grace and the forgiveness of sins on their account. For if the righteousness and the works done according to the Law do not justify, much less do sins committed against the Law justify. Therefore such people are more fortunate than the self-righteous in this respect; for they lack trust in their own works, which, even if it does not completely destroy faith in Christ, nevertheless hinders it very greatly. On the other hand, the self-righteous, who refrain from sins outwardly and seem to live blameless and religious lives, cannot avoid a presumption of confidence and righteousness, which cannot coexist with faith in Christ. Therefore they are less fortunate than tax collectors and harlots, who do not offer their good works to a wrathful God in exchange for eternal life, as the self-righteous do, since they have none to offer, but beg that their sins be forgiven them for the sake of Christ.[4]

In faith "everything of the world and the law comes to an end, and the divine begins"

Faith, conscience, and Christ
As shown above, Luther's notion of the law is marked by the idea that the law belongs only in the "world." Thus, it applies to the "old Adam," or the "flesh." But, in contrast, it must not reign in "heaven," that is, in the Christian's conscience, in which not the law but Christ—the righteousness granted by God—is to sit on the throne. He is the "law of the law," that is, freedom, and the "death of death," that is, eternal life and blessedness. The Reformer says that the conscience is like a bridal chamber, in which the bride (the believer) and the bridegroom (Christ) are left alone, and no servants (works) are allowed to be present. The servants belong in the kitchen and the rest of the house, where the happy bride serves her neighbors. Immediately, if "the devil brings works into the conscience" (that is, makes the Christian believe that works of law are a precondition for salvation), joy dies, life vanishes, and the believer becomes weak, losing his or her strength. Accordingly, Luther emphasizes that in relation to one's neighbors and to one's own flesh, i.e., the "old Adam [and Eve]"—that is, outside the domain of conscience—the law "must be made God." There, in fact, one cannot speak of it "with sufficient respect." In the conscience, however—that is, before God—the law is a "devil that brings death with it." The Reformer claims that the law and Christ are mutually contradictory and exclusive:

> Therefore let the godly person learn that the Law and Christ are mutually contradictory and altogether incompatible. When Christ is present, the Law must not rule in any way but must retreat from the conscience and yield the bed to Christ alone, since this is too narrow to hold them both (Is 28:20). Let Him rule alone in righteousness, safety, happiness, and life, so that the conscience may happily fall asleep in Christ, without any awareness of Law, sin, or death.[5]

The spiritual function of the law and the believer's participation in Christ
Even though the law belongs, in principle, in the "world" and not in "heaven," it has, however, an important task in the believer's life.

Although the law "brings death" when acting in the conscience, that is, when exercising dominion in a human being's relationship with God, it is nevertheless good "in itself" (cf. Rom. 7:12-13). When the law exercises its ministry of death, its most important spiritual function is to reveal the human being's "true face" behind the masks, and disclose his or her barefaced sinfulness. By revealing sin, the law brings death to the old Adam. This is how Luther interprets the following thought of Paul: "Sin, working death in me through what is good, in order that sin might be shown to be sin" (Rom. 7:13).

Luther says the following about the mission of the law to reveal sin and bring death:

[The Law] produces in [one] the knowledge of [oneself]. . . . Therefore the Law is a minister and a preparation for grace. For God is the God of the humble, the miserable, the afflicted, the oppressed, the desperate, and of those who have been brought down to nothing at all. And it is the nature of God to exalt the humble, to feed the hungry, to enlighten the blind, to comfort the miserable and afflicted, to justify sinners, to give life to the dead, and to save those who are desperate and damned. For He is the almighty Creator, who makes everything out of nothing.[6]

Thus, Christ is death to the death brought by the law. This idea can be compared to the following thought of Paul: "In the same way, my friends, you have died to the law through the body of Christ, so that you may belong to another, to him who has been raised from the dead in order that we may bear fruit for God" (Rom. 7:4). Furthermore, Luther also interprets the following statement of Paul from the same standpoint: "For Christ is the end of the law so that there may be righteousness for everyone who believes" (Rom. 10:4). The law implies "death" and the making of the human being into "nothing." The "darkness" and the "cloud" of faith in which Christ, in Luther's view, is really present, is therefore obviously also the kind of "darkness" and "turning into nothing" that follows from gaining self-knowledge through the law. This knowledge "brings death," that is, makes the human being "humble," "miserable," "depressed," "desperate," "naught," "dead," or "blind," as the Reformer describes this condition. It is true, however, that the "darkness" of faith does not only refer to the darkness brought by the law. That "obscurity," for example, which prevails when one believes in God's rule and providence, is also part of this darkness. On the other hand, it is nevertheless obvious that the "nothingness" and "darkness" brought about by one's self-knowledge gained through the law is an essential dimension of the "darkness" and "cloud" in which Christ is really present.

All in all, what has been said here of Luther's notion of the law confirms the point this study has been making about Luther's interpretation of the "realistic" character of faith. The law can only produce "something of the world," whereas faith is not at all a matter of the "things of the world"; in faith "everything of the world" comes to an end, and "that which is divine" begins. Luther says:

> Therefore the Law of Moses produces nothing that goes beyond the things of the world; that is, it merely shows both politically and theologically the evils that there are in the world. With its terrors it merely drives the conscience to thirst and yearn for the promise of God and to look at Christ. But for this the Holy Spirit is necessary, to say to the heart: "After the Law has performed its function in you, it is not the will of God that you merely be terrified and killed, but that you recognize your misery and your lost condition through the Law and then do not despair but believe in Christ, who is 'the end of the Law, that everyone who has faith may be justified' (Rom. 10:4)." Clearly there is nothing of the world being granted here; but everything of the world comes to an end here, and so do all the laws, while that which is divine begins.[7]

Ultimately, the "theological" function of the law is to make the human being participate through the Holy Spirit in the person of Christ and in the divine life in him—something which is entirely beyond the scope of the law as such. Thus, the Reformer's notion of the law also reveals how his Christology rests on the Christology of the early church and is "realistic" in character. There are passages in *Lectures on Galatians* where this can be seen very clearly indeed:

> Thus with the sweetest names Christ is called my Law, my sin, and my death, in opposition to the Law, sin, and death, even though in

fact He is nothing but sheer liberty, righteousness, life, and eternal salvation. Therefore He became Law to the Law, sin to sin, and death to death, in order that He might redeem me from the curse of the Law, justify me, and make me alive. And so Christ is both: While He is the Law, He is liberty; while He is sin, He is righteousness; and while he is death, He is life. For by the very fact that He permitted the Law to accuse Him, sin to damn Him, and death to devour Him He abrogated the Law, damned sin, destroyed death, and justified and saved me. *Thus Christ is a poison against the Law, sin, and death, and simultaneously a remedy to regain liberty, righteousness, and eternal life.*[8]

According to Luther, justification, when considered from the viewpoint of the work and person of Christ, happens "outside" human beings (even though it "is" also within them), and is imputed to them. However, Luther here essentially views justification from the standpoint of the person of the justified human being. From this point of view, the person of Christ *is*, in an ontologically real manner, righteousness—just as he *is* freedom and eternal life. When participating in Christ, the believer shares in an ontological and real manner in what is "death to death" (i.e., life), "sin to sin" (i.e., righteousness), and "law to the law" (i.e., freedom). This "realistic" notion of Christ also constitutes the basis for a concept which is very interesting from the viewpoint of this study and its theme: according to the Reformer, the union between the believer and Christ is so complete that these two become "one person."

Chapter 4

Christ and the Believer as One Person

s stated above, both Luther's idea of Christ as the "form" (actuality; *Seinswirklichkeit*) of faith and his notion of the law lead directly to the central theme of his theology of faith: the idea that faith means the presence of Christ and thus participation in the "divine life." Furthermore, the Reformer's exposition of the statement in Gal. 2:20, "It is no longer I who live, but it is Christ who lives in me," reveals the extent to which Luther thinks of the completeness of the union between Christ and the believer. The "old self" of the Christian dies and is replaced by the person of Christ. Christ "is in us" and "remains in us." The life that the Christian now lives *is*, in an ontologically real manner, Christ himself. At the same time it becomes apparent that Luther finds it necessary to express the relationship between Christ and the believer through the "philosophical" concept *forma*. If this relationship were given "spiritual" expression only, it would not be possible to appreciate properly this relationship's close and intimate nature. The passage referred to essentially clarifies Luther's theology of faith:

> "I do not live in my own person now, but Christ lives in me." The person does indeed live, but not in itself or for its own person. But who is this "I" of whom he says: "Yet not I"? It is the one that has the Law and is obliged to do works, the one that is a person separate from Christ. This "I" Paul rejects; for "I," as a person distinct from Christ, belongs to death and hell. This is why he says: "Not I, but Christ lives in me." Christ is my "form," which adorns my faith as color or light adorns a wall. (This fact has to be expounded in this crude way, for there is no spiritual way for us to grasp the idea that Christ clings and dwells in us as closely and intimately as light or whiteness clings to a wall.) "Christ," he

says, "is fixed and cemented to me and abides in me. The life that
I now live, He lives in me. Indeed, Christ Himself is the life that I
now live. In this way, therefore, Christ and I are one."[1]

The idea of *unio personalis* makes it obvious once again that
Luther regards the ontological nature of the presence of Christ as
absolutely real. Christ *is* freedom, righteousness, and life, and by
his presence he drives sin, death, and curse away from the believer,
making these "disappear." The Reformer says:

> Living in me as He does, Christ abolishes the Law, damns sin, and
> kills death; for at His presence all these cannot help disappear-
> ing. Christ is eternal Peace, Comfort, Righteousness, and Life,
> to which the terror of the Law, sadness of mind, sin, hell, and
> death have to yield. Abiding and living in me, Christ removes and
> absorbs all the evils that torment and afflict me. This attachment
> to Him causes me to be liberated from the terror of the Law and
> of sin, pulled out of my own skin, and transferred into Christ and
> into His kingdom, which is a kingdom of grace, righteousness,
> peace, joy, life, salvation, and eternal glory. Since I am in Him, no
> evil can harm me.[2]

Many of the subjects that are of pivotal importance to Luther
and that have already been dealt with in this study (faith as sharing
in the person of Christ; participation in the "divine nature"; faith
as the conqueror of the destructive forces of sin and evil; the
communicatio idiomatum; etc.) are given expression in the notion
of *unio*, as demonstrated, for example, in the following passage:

> Meanwhile my old man (Eph. 4:22) remains outside and is sub-
> ject to the Law. But so far as justification is concerned, Christ and
> I must be so closely attached that He lives in me and I in Him.
> What a marvelous way of speaking! Because He lives in me, what-
> ever grace, righteousness, life, peace, and salvation there is in me is
> all Christ's; nevertheless, it is mine as well, by the cementing and
> attachment that are through faith, by which we become as one body
> in the Spirit. Since Christ lives in me, grace, righteousness, life, and
> eternal salvation must be present with Him; and the Law, sin, and

death must be absent. Indeed, the Law must be crucified, devoured, and abolished by the Law—and sin by sin, death by death, the devil by the devil. In this way Paul seeks to withdraw us completely from ourselves, from the Law, and from works, and to transplant us into Christ and faith in Christ, so that in the area of justification we look only at grace, and separate it far from the Law and from works, which belong far away.[3]

The *unio personalis* is perhaps the most intensive of the expressions Luther uses to describe the union between Christ and the believer. This image, which is close to mysticism,[4] is an integral part of Luther's doctrine of justification. The idea of personal union is not to be regarded as a provisional or incidental exaggeration in Luther, who often emphasizes the idea of the *unio* precisely when polemicizing the scholastic notion of justification. This idea of the union of persons thus points to something essential in the Reformer's theology. Luther says:

> But faith must be taught correctly, namely, that by it you are so cemented to Christ that He and you are as one person, which cannot be separated but remains attached to Him forever and declares: "I am as Christ." And Christ, in turn, says: "I am that sinner who is attached to Me, and I to him. For by faith we are joined together into one flesh and one bone." Thus Eph. 5:30 says: "We are members of the body of Christ, of His flesh and of His bones," in such a way that this faith couples Christ and me more intimately than a husband is coupled to his wife. Therefore this faith is no idle quality; but it is a thing of such magnitude that it obscures and completely removes those foolish dreams of the sophists' doctrine—the fiction of a "formed faith" and of love, of merits, our worthiness, our quality, etc.[5]

There is no doubt that the idea of the believer's real participation in Christ is an essential part of Luther's theology of justification. At least on the level of terminology, the distinction between justification and the divine indwelling in the believer, made by the *Formula of Concord* and by the major part of later Lutheran theology, is alien to the Reformer. There is a passage in Luther's *Lectures on Galatians* in which he seems to explicitly refute this later notion, even though the actual point of his polemic is directed against the *fides charitate formata* position specifically. The Reformer claims that if the person of Christ and that of the believer are separated from each other in the doctrine of justification, salvation is still being considered within the framework of the order of the law, which means being "dead in the sight of God":

> It is unprecedented and insolent to say: "I live, I do not live; I am dead, I am not dead; I am a sinner, I am not a sinner; I have the Law, I do not have the Law." But this phraseology is true in Christ and through Christ. *When it comes to justification, therefore, if you divide Christ's Person from your own, you are in the Law; you remain in it and live in yourself, which means that you are dead in the sight of God and damned by the Law.*[6]

In faith, the person of Christ and that of the believer are made one, and this oneness must not be divided; what is at stake here is salvation, or the loss of it. In the *Formula of Concord*, on the other hand, justification is defined only as the imputation of the forgiveness of sins, whereas *inhabitatio Dei* is defined as a separate phenomenon and part of sanctification or renewal.

Luther does not hesitate to conclude that in faith the human being becomes "God," not in substance but through participation. This notion, which has been forgotten in Protestant theology, is an integral part of Luther's theology of faith, if interpreted correctly.

Chapter 5

"Through Faith One Becomes God"

The Christian as a "divine human being"

It is not only in terms of its meaning that Luther is familiar with the notion of participation in the divine life. He also refers to the doctrine of divinization terminologically, as mentioned in the introduction to this study. In so doing, he usually relies on the same biblical quotation on which the patristic doctrine of divinization was also based. It is true that in his *Lectures on Galatians* the Reformer does not refer to the doctrine of *theopoiesis* very often, as far as terminology is concerned; on the other hand, neither does the commentary lack such points of contact. Thus, Luther says the following when analyzing the relationship between faith and love: "faith makes a [person] God (2 Peter 1:4)."[1] Moreover, he states that the union between Christ and the believer makes the latter a "completely divine [person]." Because of the real presence of Christ in Christians, they are also themselves victors over the destructive forces of sin and evil. Luther says:

> The one who has faith is a completely divine man, a son of God, the inheritor of the universe. He is the victor over the world, sin, death, and the devil. Hence he cannot be praised enough.

> Therefore the Abraham who has faith fills heaven and earth; thus every Christian fills heaven and earth by his faith.[2]

Faith has (possesses) Christ "as a ring has a gem." Therefore believers, who have this "small gift" in their conscience, are greater than "heaven and earth, the law, the devil, and death." In the eyes of human beings, this gift, Christ, is small, but its smallness is "greater than the entire world."[3]

Owing to this gift, that is, Christ, Christians have a unique position among all creatures. They become "lords over everything," even over sin and death. Furthermore, Luther's notion of the participation of Christians in the priesthood and kingship of all believers is based on the conception of the presence of Christ. Thus, one of Luther's main reformatory treatises of the 1520s, *The Freedom of a Christian,* has a classic passage that becomes readily understandable in light of the notion of *Christus praesens*:

> Now just as Christ by his birthright obtained these two prerogatives [priesthood and kingship], so he imparts them to and shares them with everyone who believes in him. . . . Hence all of us who believe in Christ are priests and kings in Christ, as I Pet. 2[:9] says: "You are . . . a royal priesthood, a priestly kingdom." . . . With respect to the kingship, every Christian is by faith so exalted above all things that, by virtue of a spiritual power, he is lord of all things without exception, so that nothing can do him any harm. As a matter of fact, all things are made subject to him and are compelled to serve him in obtaining salvation. Accordingly Paul says in Rom. 8[:28], "All things work together for good for the elect," and in I Cor. 3[:21-23], "All things are yours whether . . . life or death or the present or the future, all are yours."[4]

Furthermore, because of the presence of Christ, the Christian becomes a "wonderful creator." Luther says,

> A Christian becomes a skillful artisan and a wonderful creator, who can make joy out of sadness, comfort out of terror, righteousness out of sin, and life out of death.[5]

The Lutheran form of the doctrine of divinization also finds expression in passages where Luther explains that faith means that human beings are given the form of Christ. In faith, Christians receive the likeness of God's image (*imago*). They have the form (*forma*) and likeness (*similitudo*) of God. According to Luther, the transformation of a human being into the likeness of God means precisely the following: *a lege in fidem Christi* (from the law to faith in Christ).[6] And the reason for faith denoting a human being's transformation into the likeness of God is that Christ is present in faith and communicates his divine attributes to this human being. This becomes very obvious in light of a passage from the *Church Postil* (already referred to earlier):

> And so we are filled with "all the fullness of God." This phrase, which follows the Hebrew manner of speaking, means that we are filled in all the ways in which He fills a [person]. *We are filled with God,* and He pours into us all His gifts and grace and fills us with His Spirit, who makes us courageous. He enlightens us with His light, His life lives in us, His beatitude makes us blessed, and His love causes love to arise in us. Put briefly, He fills us in order that *everything that He is and everything He can do might be in us in all its fullness, and work powerfully, so that we might be divinized throughout*—not having only a small part of God, or merely some parts of Him, but having all His fullness. Much has been written on the divinization of man, and ladders have been constructed by means of which man is to ascend to heaven, and many other things of this kind have been done. However, all these are merely works of a beggar. What must be done instead is to show the right and straight way to *your being filled with God,* so that you do not lack any part but have it all gathered together, and so that all you say, all you think and everywhere you go—in sum, *all your life—is throughout divine.*[7]

In this passage, Luther maintains—in a manner mostly forgotten in Luther research—that faith denotes the true and complete "divinization" of a human being. By contrast, the *fides charitate formata* position, which rests on Greek ontology and its notion of striving love, only signifies a partial, incomplete, and insufficient divinization. The relationship of a human being with God is seen in this view as an incessant movement toward transcendence—that is, toward God, who nevertheless remains in "heaven." According to Luther, however, the true faith unites the Christian with God who in God's *agape*-love has "descended" to us and who is present in the sinner by being present in faith in all God's fullness. Faith is "heaven."

The concept of divinization and the relationship between faith and works

The significance of the concept of divinization for Luther's doctrine of justification culminates in his view that the relationship between faith and works is analogous to that between Christ's divine and human nature. Christ, who is present in faith, is the form who informs works, that is, becomes incarnate in them.

> Therefore in theology let faith always be the divinity of works, diffused throughout the works in the same way that the divinity is throughout the humanity of Christ. Anyone who touches the heat in the heated iron touches the iron; and whoever has touched the skin of Christ has actually touched God. Therefore faith is the "do-all" in works, if I may use this expression.[8]

According to Luther, faith is "form" and works are "matter." The Christ who is present in faith informs the works, that is, becomes incarnate in them (*fides composita, fides concreta, fides incarnata*).[9] When the reality of faith becomes incarnate in works they become works made into faith (*opera fideificata*)—or, as Luther says explicitly, "divinized works" (*opera deificata*).[10]

Thus, the concept of *deificatio* is at the very heart of the Reformer's doctrine of justification. On this basis, it is evident that the doctrine of justification and the idea of sanctification constitute one whole in Luther's theology.

Part II

THE PRESENCE
OF CHRIST IN FAITH
AND THE HOLINESS
OF CHRISTIANS

Chapter 6

The Presence of Christ and Sanctification

Christ as the subject of good works

The strict distinction between justification and sanctification that came to characterize later Lutheran theology is not at all a central or constitutive distinction in the theology of Luther. Rather, the way in which these concepts have been set against each other goes back to the questions and problems typical of Lutheran argumentation after Melanchthon, and of the *Formula of Concord*. An important background for this argumentation is the stir created by Andreas Osiander's teaching concerning justification and divine indwelling. In mainstream Lutheran tradition, the remission of sins, on the one hand, and the *inhabitatio* of God in the believer, on the other, are separated from each other terminologically, as stated earlier in this study: only the former is called justification, whereas the latter term is used for renewal (*renovatio*) and sanctification (*sanctificatio*). Luther's view of the relationship between justification and sanctification, which is analyzed here, lends a perspective for looking at the distinction from the center that unites the two: this center is the notion of Christ who is present in faith.

The logic of the Reformer's thinking is as follows: *In faith, human beings are really united with Christ. Christ, in turn, is both the forgiveness of sins and the effective producer of everything that is good in them.* Therefore "sanctification"—that is, the sanctity or holiness of the Christian—is, in fact, only another name for the same phenomenon of which Luther speaks when discussing the communication of attributes, the happy exchange, and the union between the person of Christ and that of the believer. Christ is the true subject and agent of good works in the believer, as illustrated, for example, by the following passage:

"There is a double life: my own, which is natural or animate; and an alien life, that of Christ in me. So far as my animate life is concerned, I am dead and am now living an alien life. I am not living as Paul now, for Paul is dead." "Who, then, is living?" "The Christian." Paul, living in himself, is utterly dead through the Law but living in Christ, or rather with Christ living in him, he lives an alien life. Christ is speaking, acting, and performing all actions in him.[1]

Christ is, thus, the true agent of good works in the Christian. This is how Luther interprets the words of Paul about the life that Christians now live "in the flesh," that is, in this age—it is "by faith in the Son of God." Faith means, as stated repeatedly above, the real presence of the person and work of Christ. Because of the Christian's union with Christ, his or her works are works of Christ himself. Thus, the Reformer thinks that the "word" uttered by the believer is not "the word of the flesh" but "the Word of the Holy Spirit and of Christ." In the same way, the vision that enters the eyes of the Christian does not "come from the flesh" but is directed by "the Holy Spirit." In like manner, "hearing" does not "come from the flesh," either, but is "in and from the Holy Spirit." In this argumentation Luther's view of Christians as "Christs to their neighbors" finds its ontological realization. Luther argues that Christ who is present in faith becomes, as it were, incarnate in Christians' works.

"Therefore," says Paul, "whatever this life is that I now live in the flesh, I live by faith in the Son of God." That is, the Word I speak physically is not the word of the flesh; it is the Word of the Holy Spirit and of Christ. The vision that enters or leaves my eyes does not come from the flesh; that is, my flesh does not direct it, but the Holy Spirit does. Thus hearing does not come from the flesh, even though it is in the flesh; but it is in and from the Holy Spirit. A Christian speaks nothing but chaste, sober, holy, and divine things—things that pertain to Christ, the glory of God, and the salvation of his neighbor. These things do not come from the flesh, nor are they done according to the flesh; nevertheless, they are in the flesh. I cannot teach, preach, write, pray, or give thanks except by these physical instruments, which are required for the performance of these activities. Nevertheless, these activities do not come from the flesh and do not originate there; they are given and revealed divinely from heaven. Thus also I look at a woman with my eyes, yet with a chaste vision and not in desire for her. Such vision does not come from the flesh, even though it is in the flesh; the eyes are the physical instrument of the vision, but the chastity of the vision comes from heaven.[2]

Thus, Luther holds that the new conduct of believers—when they take their neighbor into account and are willing to act in their neighbors' best interest—is based on the fact that the one who exercises dominion over Christians' hearts is Christ, who "sees, hears, speaks, works, suffers, and does simply everything" in their hearts, even though "the flesh is still reluctant." The notion of *inhabitatio Christi* is thus connected with Luther's concept of sanctification.

From all this it is evident whence this alien and spiritual life comes. The unspiritual man does not perceive this, because he does not know what sort of life this is. He "hears the sound of the wind, but he does not know whence it comes or whither it goes" (John 3:8). He hears the voice of the spiritual man; he recognizes his face, his habits, and his gestures. But whence these words come, which are not sacrilegious or blasphemous now but holy and divine, and whence these motives and actions come—this he does not see. For this life is in the heart through faith. There the flesh is extinguished; and there Christ rules with His Holy Spirit, who now sees, hears, speaks, works, suffers, and does simply everything in him, even though the flesh is still reluctant. In short, this life is not the life of the flesh, although it is a life in the flesh; but it is the life of Christ, the Son of God, whom the Christian possesses by faith.[3]

The role of the Christ present in faith as the true source of the Christian's holiness finds a concrete illustration in the parable of a tree and its fruit, which Luther uses frequently and which presents the same subject matter from a new point of view.

The parable of a tree:
A new person bearing good fruit is created "in faith"

The parable of a tree makes evident the real, almost physically natural quality of the holiness that a human being, in Luther's view, receives in faith. The starting point for the Reformer's view is the idea presented in the New Testament according to which a "tree" must first become good, and only then can it bear "good fruit." The essence, or "juice," or "substance" of the tree must change.[4] This takes place in justifying faith, in which Christ comes into the human being. Thus, faith creates a new "tree," that is, a new "person," which bears good fruit.

As constructed with the parable of a tree and its fruit, the definition of the relationship between faith and works, in Luther's opinion, marks the division between the philosophical ethic and the theological ethic. The former teaches that human beings become righteous by performing righteous works. Theology, by contrast, teaches differently: it says that the justified, that is, those who are in Christ through faith, perform righteous works. Luther says:

> Thus he is a true doer of the Law who receives the Holy Spirit through faith in Christ and then begins to love God and to do good to his neighbor. Hence "to do" includes faith at the same time. Faith takes the doer himself and makes him into a tree, and his deeds become fruit. First there must be a tree, then the fruit. For apples do not make a tree, but a tree makes apples. So faith first makes the person, who afterward performs works. To keep the Law without faith, therefore, is to make apples without a tree, out of wood or mud, which is not to make apples but to make mere phantasies. But once the tree has been planted, that is, once there is the person or doer who comes into being through faith in Christ, then works follow.[5]

Luther's interpretation of the parable of the tree and its fruits also allows a definite conclusion on what Luther means by his idea (mentioned earlier) that faith and works, on the one hand, and the divine and human nature of Christ, on the other, are in an analogous relation to each other. Both images speak to the same issue:

A theological work is a work done in faith; thus a theological [person] is a [person] of faith. In like manner, a right reason and a good will are a reason and will in faith. *Thus faith is universally the divinity in the work, the person, and the members of the body, as the one and only cause of justification*; afterwards this is attributed to the matter on account of the form, to the work on account of the faith. The kingly authority of the divinity is given to Christ the man, not because of His humanity but because of His divinity. For the divinity alone created all things, without the cooperation of the humanity. Nor did the humanity conquer sin and death; but the hook that was concealed under the worm, at which the devil struck, conquered and devoured the devil, who was attempting to devour the worm. Therefore the humanity would not have accomplished anything by itself; but the divinity, joined with the humanity, did it alone, and the humanity did it on account of the divinity. So here faith alone justifies and does everything; nevertheless, it is attributed to works on account of faith.[6]

Faith, which works in the Christian, is "the one and only cause of justification." Thus, according to the idea of the real presence of Christ, faith and works relate to each other in the same way as Christ's divine nature relates to his human nature, and vice versa. Luther applies thus the Chalcedonian christological formula to the relationship between faith and works:

Therefore faith always justifies and makes alive; and yet it does not remain alone, that is, idle. Not that it does not remain alone on its own level and in its own function, for it always justifies alone. But it is incarnate and becomes man; that is, it neither is nor remains idle or without love. Thus Christ, according to His divinity, is a divine and eternal essence or nature, without a beginning; but His humanity is a nature created in time. These two natures in Christ are not confused or mixed, and the properties of each must be clearly understood. It is characteristic of the humanity to have a beginning in time, but it is characteristic of the divinity to be eternal and without a beginning. Nevertheless, these two are combined, and the divinity without a beginning is incorporated into the humanity with a beginning. Just as I am obliged to distinguish between the humanity and the divinity, and to say: "The humanity is not the divinity, and yet the man is God," so I make a distinction here and say: "The Law is not faith, and yet faith does works. Faith and works are in agreement concretely or compositely, and yet each has and preserves its own nature and proper function."[7]

The parallelism of the doctrines of justification and divinization culminates in the analogous constitution of Christ and the believer. This analogy also makes understandable many of Luther's characteristic reformatory ideas. To Luther, faith is the "divinity" that becomes incarnate in works (in the published text of Luther's *Lectures on Galatians,* the concept "beautiful incarnation," *pulchra incarnatio,* is used for this); therefore, sanctification, in regard to both the will and the intellect of the Christian, comes solely from Christ who is present and works in faith. Our knowledge of God is something "created in us" rather than something "we have created." It is more appropriate to say that "we are known" by God than that "we know" God.[8] In like manner, our "doing" or action is to "permit God to do His work in us." Furthermore, "good works do not grow in our garden." Thus, justification and "sanctification" are extremely closely united in the theology of Luther. The true agent of good works and the person performing them is Christ, who is present in faith. The beautiful allegory used by the Reformer that depicts Christ as the Good Samaritan also expresses the idea that the true agent of sanctification is none other than Christ:

We are that wounded man who fell among robbers; whose wounds the Samaritan bound up, pouring on oil and wine; whom he set on his own beast and brought to an inn and took care of; and whom he entrusted to the innkeeper upon departing, with the words: "Take care of him" (Luke 10:30-35). Thus we are cherished meanwhile as in an inn, until the Lord reaches out His hand a second time, as Isaiah says, to deliver us.[9]

Chapter 7

"Simultaneously Righteous and a Sinner"

The "real righteousness" and "imputation" (declaration of righteousness)

The allegory of Christ as the Good Samaritan, the healer of the wounded man who had been beaten up, immediately brings up a question: to what extent is a Christian really *made* righteous in justification, and to what extent is justification merely an imputation (*imputatio; reputatio; Gerechterklärung*), in which the sinner is *declared* righteous? This question makes it possible to recognize once again the fact that the notion of *in ipsa fide Christus adest* is the key to the fundamental structure of the Reformer's thinking.[1]

According to Luther, there are two factors constituting "Christian righteousness," namely, the "faith in the heart" and the "imputation of God."[2] They relate to each other in the following way, to give a preliminary definition: faith is, in itself, a real righteousness (*fides est iustitia formalis*),[3] even though it is, on the other hand, only initial righteousness. Namely, because faith is "weak," believers still have much sin in their "flesh," in their "old Adam." Because of these remaining sins it is necessary for justification that God "imputes" the righteousness of Christ to Christians. Luther says:

> Now acceptance or imputation is extremely necessary, first, because we are not yet purely righteous, but sin is still clinging to our flesh during this life. God cleanses this remnant of sin in our flesh. In addition, we are sometimes forsaken by the Holy Spirit, and we fall into sins, as did Peter, David, and other saints. Nevertheless, we always have recourse to this doctrine, that our sins are covered and that God does not want to impute them to us (Rom. 4). This

does not mean that there is no sin in us, as the sophists have taught when they said that we must go on doing good until we are no longer conscious of any sin; but sin is always present, and the godly feel it. But it is ignored and hidden in the sight of God, because Christ the Mediator stands between; because we take hold of Him by faith, all our sins are sins no longer.[4]

Thus, Luther's fundamental idea can be expressed by saying that faith is the beginning of real righteousness, while through imputation this initial righteousness is "perfected" as long as one lives in this age. "*Fides ergo incipit, reputatio perficit usque ad illum diem.*"[5] It is because of the imperfectness of faith that imputation is necessary. Luther says:

Make now the following distinction: "Faith is imputed to him as righteousness for the sake of Christ." 1. Faith is a divinely granted gift, through which I believe in Christ. 2. God reckons this imperfect faith as perfect righteousness. God sets before His eyes the suffering Christ, in whom I have begun to believe. As long as I live in the flesh, there is sin in me, but God does not see it because of my faith in Christ: between Him and me there is a ceiling called the remission of sins, preventing God from seeing the sins. I am a sinner, my flesh is angry with God and does not rejoice in Him, and I am furious. But God does not know of these sins; I am in them, but as if they were not sins. This is accomplished by imputation.[6]

This quoted passage, however, immediately gives rise to the question of the roles of faith and Christ in the imputation. To begin with, it is obvious that Luther is familiar with the forensic aspect of justification and, related to that, the idea of the imputation of righteousness to the sinner for the sake of Christ. However, Luther's view is not simply and solely forensic, and so he says, for example: "To take hold of the Son and to believe in Him with the heart as the gift of God *causes* God (*bringt zustande, hoc facit*) to reckon *that faith* . . . as . . . righteousness."[7] Thus, faith is also, in a certain sense, a basis (*hoc facit*) for the imputation. Does this mean, then, that in Luther's opinion human beings are not justified for Christ's sake *alone* but also on account of something which is within themselves (i.e., faith)?

The answer to this question can be found in the fundamental idea in Luther's theology: According to Luther's basic view, Christ is, without separation and without confusion, *both* God's favor (*favor*) *and* God's gift (*donum*). Christ as the "favor" signifies the heart of God that is merciful to the human being, i.e., God's forgiveness, and the removal of God's wrath. The concept of "gift," in turn, denotes the real presence of Christ, and thus it also means that through Christ the believer is made a participant in the "divine nature," that is, in righteousness, life, salvation ("happiness"), power, blessing, and so forth. However, while being present, Christ is also at the same time God's favor (*favor*), forgiveness. We are not justified for the sake of anything that originates "from us," but for the sake of Christ, who is present in us in faith. Christ is our justification and sanctification.

The idea of *in ipsa fide Christus adest* well explicates the relationship between "righteous-making" and "imputation." *Faith is the basis for justification precisely because faith means the real presence of the person of Christ, that is, the real presence of God's favor and gift.* In other words: *The Christ who dwells in faith in Christians is the Christian righteousness that God imputes to them.* The Reformer says this explicitly:

> Therefore faith justifies because it takes hold of and possesses this treasure, the present Christ. But how He is present—this is beyond our thought; for there is darkness, as I have said. Where the confidence of the heart is present, therefore, there Christ is present, in that very cloud and faith. This is the formal righteousness on account of which a man is justified; it is not on account of love, as the sophists say. In short, just as the sophists say that love forms and fulfills faith, so we say that it is Christ who forms and fulfills faith or who is the form of faith. *Therefore the Christ who is grasped by faith and who lives in the heart is the true Christian righteousness, on account of which God counts us righteous* and grants us eternal life. Here there is no work of the Law, no love; but there is an entirely different kind of righteousness, a new world above and beyond the Law. For Christ or faith is neither the Law nor the work of the Law.[8]

Luther even says that the faith that unites the Christian with Christ is the basis and reason (*ratio*)[9] for the imputation:

> Here it is to be noted that these three things are joined together: faith, Christ, and acceptance or imputation. Faith takes hold of Christ and has Him present, enclosing Him as the ring encloses the gem. And whoever is found having this faith in the Christ who is grasped in the heart, him God accounts as righteous. *This is the cause [ratio] and the merit by which we obtain the forgiveness of sins and righteousness.* "Because you believe in Me," God says, "and your faith takes hold of Christ, whom I have freely given to you as your Justifier and Savior, therefore be righteous." Thus God accepts you or accounts you righteous only on account of Christ, in whom you believe.[10]

The idea *in ipsa fide Christus adest* is the key, thus, not only to the problem of the relationship between "righteous-making" and imputation, but also to Luther's view on how Christians are, not only "partially" but also "totally," simultaneously righteous and sinners.

The partial and the total aspects of justification

In Luther research, scholars have labored to find out what the Reformer means when he speaks of Christians as totally righteous and total sinners. By contrast, the partial aspect—Christians as partly righteous and partly sinners—has frequently been left without the attention that it nevertheless deserves.

When Luther talks about Christians from the "total" point of view, he considers them in a relationship with the one who is "outside" them even when he is "in them," namely, Christ. Christians are "totally righteous" in their relationship with the one "above," that is, with Christ and God. On the other hand, Christians are to be understood as "total sinners" in themselves, when they are seen as the "old Adam [Eve]," and separate from Christ.

When talking about the partial aspect of justification, Luther's attention is focused on believers themselves and on the battle between the new and the old in them. Luther states explicitly that

Christians live "partly in the flesh and partly in the Spirit" (*partim carnem, partim Spiritum habent*), which means that they are partly sinners and partly righteous. The "flesh," or the "old Adam," has certainly not died in Christians, and will not die in this life. The flesh is opposed to the "Spirit," and the "Spirit" is opposed to the flesh. However, in the course of this battle the present Christ "sweeps" the old Adam [Eve] away and "cleanses" believers.

The patristic image of Christ as leaven illustrates in a particularly concrete manner Christ's role and work in the conflict between the flesh and the Spirit. The image of leaven is also used by Luther:

> Thus we have received the first fruits of the Spirit (Rom. 8:23), and the leaven hidden in the lump; the whole lump has not yet been leavened, but it is beginning to be leavened. If I look at the leaven, I see nothing but the leaven; but if I look at the mass of the lump, it is not yet totally permeated by the leaven. Thus if I look at Christ, I am completely holy and pure, and I know nothing at all about the Law; for Christ is my leaven. But if I look at my flesh, I feel greed, lust, anger, pride, the terror of death, sadness, fear, hate, grumbling, and impatience against God. To the extent that these are present, Christ is absent; or if He is present, He is present weakly. Here there is still need for a custodian to discipline and torment the flesh, that powerful jackass, so that by this discipline sins may be diminished and the way prepared for Christ. For just as Christ came once physically, according to time, abrogating the entire Law, abolishing sin, and destroying death and hell, so He comes to us spiritually without interruption and continually smothers and kills these things in us.[11]

This passage shows how the concept of the presence of Christ in faith makes understandable Luther's view of Christians as partly righteous and partly sinners: Christ did not come to us only once, historically, but he comes incessantly, in the spirit, and removes sin from the believer. To use a patristic, realistic image, Christ is regarded as leaven which is to permeate the whole dough, that is, the old Adam [Eve]. (It is not a coincidence that the idea of "leaven" is also an integral part of the patristic doctrine of *theopoiesis*.) The concrete and real being of the Christ-leaven in a human being is indisputably evident in Luther's statement that to the extent there is still sin in the believer, to that extent Christ is not yet present. Hence, leavening is a process that will not be completed until the believer is raised from the dead with Christ.

> It is true that if you consider Christ, the Law and sin have really been abolished. But Christ has not yet come to you; or if He has come, there are still remnants of sin in you, and you have not yet been completely leavened. For where there is lust, sadness of heart, fear of death, and the like, there the Law and sin are still present; there Christ is not yet present. For when He comes, He drives out fear and sadness, and brings peace and security to the conscience. To the extent that I take hold of Christ by faith, there-fore, to that extent the Law has been abrogated for me. But my flesh, the world, and the devil do not permit faith to be perfect. I would, of course, wish that the little light of my faith that is in my heart might be diffused through my whole body and all its members. But this does not happen; it is not diffused all at once, but it has begun to be diffused. Meanwhile our comfort is that we have the first fruits of the Spirit and have begun to be leavened, [and] that we shall be completely leavened when this sinful body is destroyed and we arise new with Christ. Amen.[12]

However, the concept of the real presence of Christ in faith explains not only the *partim-partim* aspect but also the "total" perspective, namely, the concept of Christians as totally righteous and total sinners. Here believers are not viewed in regard to the battle they experience between the new and the old, but in their relationship with the one outside them, namely, Christ.

Naturally, the *totus-totus* aspect finds its explanation in the perspective of imputation, which we have discussed above: God does not take into account the sins remaining in Christians, but forgives these sins for the sake of Christ, in whom Christians believe and who is present in them. Luther often explains the total aspect from the idea of *imputatio*, as in the following text:

> To take hold of the Son and to believe in Him with the heart as the gift of God causes God to reckon that faith, however imperfect it

may be, as perfect righteousness. Here we are in an altogether different world—a world that is outside reason. Here the issue is not what we ought to do or by what sort of works we may merit grace and the forgiveness of sins. No, here we are in a divine theology, where we hear the Gospel that Christ died for us and that when we believe this we are reckoned as righteous, even though sins, and great ones at that, still remain in us.[13]

The meaning of the "total" aspect of justification can be understood not only from the idea of imputation but also from Luther's teaching of Christ as a "gift." The "leavening" is and *remains* the work of Christ *himself,* whose presence in faith is real. While Christ indeed cleanses Christians more and more through the remission of sins and, from that basis, through the knowledge of Christ, if the Spirit of Christ were to abandon believers, they would find themselves again in the same condition in which they were before Christ came to them. This line of thought shows the connection between the notion of Christ as a gift and the "total" aspect of justification: in themselves, without Christ, Christians are sinners, but in the gift of Christ they are truly and really righteous. This view is expressed, for example, in the following passage:

Now we . . . have this noble knowledge of Christ: Where He is recognized as the one who helps and gives the strength to fulfill the Law and through whom we have received the forgiveness of sins, there His glory is reflected in us. Christ is reflected in the same way as the sunlight is reflected in the water or in a mirror, and He lets Himself shine in our hearts. So we will be glorified, from glory to glory, so that we grow daily and get to know the Lord more and more clearly. Thus we are transformed and glorified into His very image, so that we become one cake with Christ. We cannot make this happen by our own strength; God, who is the Spirit, must do it. Namely, if the Holy Spirit already saw this glory and light in us, and then left us, we would be as before.[14]

Chapter 8

The Christian Struggle

The "desires of the flesh":
A fight against faith and neighborly love

According to Luther, a harsh and continuous struggle is incessantly
going on in Christians because the "flesh," or the "old Adam," still
remains in them. In the interpretation of this fight, the notion of
participation in the divine life in Christ proves to be essentially
important, once again. Namely, the fight against the flesh is fought
in the power of "the Spirit of Christ." Luther grounds this idea on
the norm introduced by Paul: "Live by the Spirit . . . , and do not
gratify the desires of the flesh" (Gal. 5:16). In order to understand
the battle between the flesh and the Spirit, we must first clarify the
content of the "desires of the flesh."

In Luther's theology, the definition of the desires of the flesh is
based on the question of whom or what these desires fight against.
Ultimately and fundamentally, the desires of the flesh concentrate
on one thing only: they fight against the Spirit of Christ. This
means that in "desiring," the flesh tries to abolish two things: faith
in Christ and love of one's neighbor.[1]

Luther is of the opinion that Christian life, in its entirety,
consists of two things: faith and love.[2] Faith belongs to the
relationship of human beings with God, whereas love belongs in
this context to their relationships with their neighbors. Both are
equally important[3] and belong integrally together. Both must be
given an equal amount of space in the teaching of the church. It
is true, however, that faith constitutes the basis, because it is in
faith that the "new person" who bears good fruit is planted, as we
have shown earlier. However, faith, on the other hand, teaches
Christians what true love for their neighbor means, and enables
them to realize it. Because Christians no longer have to "perform

works" in order to achieve salvation through them, their works are freed for the exclusive service of their neighbors. Earlier in this study, faith as one of the opponents of the desires of the flesh was discussed; it is also necessary to characterize briefly the other principal "enemy" of these desires, that is, neighborly love.

According to Luther, the need of the neighbor is the ultimate criterion and norm for one's love of one's neighbor. Luther states that this principle has been formulated in the so-called "Golden Rule," the briefest form of which reads: love your neighbor as yourself. This rule means that all human beings are in principle able to know what other people need, by putting themselves in the place of others and considering what these would wish in each situation. Luther says:

> It is a brief statement, expressed beautifully and forcefully: "You shall love your neighbor as yourself." No one can find a better, surer, or more available pattern than himself; nor can there be a nobler or more profound attitude of the mind than love; nor is there a more excellent object than one's neighbor. Therefore the pattern, the attitude, and the object are all superb. Thus if you want to know how the neighbor is to be loved and want to have an outstanding pattern of this, consider carefully how you love yourself. In need or in danger you would certainly want desperately to be loved and assisted with all the counsels, resources, and powers not only of all men but of all creation. And so you do not need any book to instruct and admonish you how you should love your neighbor, for you have the loveliest and best of books about all laws right in your own heart. You do not need any teacher to tell you about this matter; merely consult your own heart, and it will give you abundant instruction that you should love your neighbor as you love yourself. What is more, love is the highest virtue. It is ready to be of service not only with its tongue, its hands, its money, and its abilities but with its body and its very life.[4]

Besides being opposed to faith, the desires of the flesh also seek to fight against the neighborly love described above. "Desire" does not signify sensual lust. Rather, Luther says that all affects that are opposed to faith and neighborly love belong to the domain of the flesh. Thus, he also calls mental phenomena "lusts of the flesh." Among these are unbelief, despair, blasphemy, bitterness, fear of death, melancholy, sluggishness, hatred, impudence, arrogance, ambition, contempt for one's neighbor, anger, lack of love, heresy, factions, strife, neglect of God's word, and so forth.

Because Christians continue to be "partly righteous" and "partly sinners" in themselves, they still have remnants of the desires of the flesh in them. This remaining sin—even though not considered, or imputed against Christians, owing to God's forgiveness—is still effective in them. Thus, Christians must live by the Spirit, in order not to "gratify" the desires of the flesh. This does not happen, however, without a struggle: the flesh and the Spirit fight against each other in believers. In other words, faith and love fight together against unbelief and lack of love.

It should be noted that, according to Luther, the mortification of the flesh is needed for the realization of faith and love; thus, it is not a goal in itself. Christians must watch for their "old Adam [Eve]" in order to be able to believe and love.

"Progress" in the struggle between the flesh and the Spirit

Luther usually describes the struggle in which the flesh is opposed to the Spirit and the Spirit to the flesh by saying that from the human being's point of view this struggle looks like slow and unsuccessful "crawling." Nevertheless, owing to the greatness of the Christ present in faith, this fight is, in fact, successful "running." The following description of this battle is characteristic of Luther. A point to which attention should be paid here is the central position occupied by the notion of *in ipsa fide Christus adest*. Christ is present in faith, and he is, firstly, a gift. He communicates his attributes to the Christian. (In the following quotation, Christ is described as "holy," "righteous," and "joyful," and there is nothing that believers lack in him, either.) On the other hand, the concept of Christ as the "favor" also emerges in the passage as a secondary theme: Luther supposes all the time that God "reckons" the "slow" fight as fast running. Both aspects belong inseparably together. Luther says:

But the words "You were running well" contain comfort. For with these words Paul pays attention to the trial by which the devout are disciplined; to themselves their life seems dreary, closer to crawling than to running. But when there is sound teaching—which cannot be without results, since it brings the Holy Spirit and His gifts—the life of the devout is strenuous running, even though it may seem to be crawling. To us, of course, it seems that everything is moving ahead slowly and with great difficulty; but what seems slow to us is rapid in the sight of God, and what hardly crawls for us runs swiftly for Him. Likewise, what is sorrow, sin, and death in our eyes is joy, righteousness, and life in the eyes of God, for the sake of Christ, through whom we are made perfect. Christ is holy, righteous, joyful, etc., and there is nothing that He lacks; thus there is nothing that believers in Him lack either. Therefore Christians are really runners; whatever they do runs along and moves forward successfully, being advanced by the Spirit of Christ, who has nothing to do with slow enterprises.[5]

However, in addition to the notion of the progress that is seemingly "slow" but "fast" in reality, the Reformer is familiar with the idea that the struggle between the "flesh" and the Spirit of Christ has advanced to different stages in different believers. In some of them, the rule of the Spirit has proceeded further than in others. In some of them, the "leaven" has permeated the "dough" of the flesh more thoroughly than in their fellow Christians. Nevertheless, when believers are viewed from the perspective of their relationship with God, all are on the same footing—that is, all are saved by grace alone and are totally righteous before God only in Christ. From this point of view, the Virgin Mary has no preferential position in comparison with the weakest member of the church. However, from the point of view of the fight between the Spirit and the flesh in believers themselves, there are differences between individuals. For example, Luther maintains that St. Peter had been cleansed and "cleaned" by the Holy Spirit much more thoroughly than Luther himself.[6]

Thus, it is obvious that, according to Luther, some kind of "progress" (*profectus*) can take place in the Christian. This idea is included in the basic concept itself, according to which the presence of Christ in faith means the beginning of a real transformation. However, in spite of the fact that the notion of transformation is an integral part of the entirety of Luther's thinking, it must be noted that it is always the *beginning* that is concerned. Among other things, Luther says:

> Shaded and protected by this covering, this heaven of the forgiveness of sins and this mercy seat, we begin to love and to keep the Law. As long as we live, we are not justified or accepted by God on account of this keeping of the Law. But "when Christ delivers the kingdom to God the Father after destroying every authority" (1 Cor. 15:24), and when "God is everything to everyone" (1 Cor. 15:28), then faith and hope will pass away, and love will be perfect and eternal (1 Cor. 13:8).[7]

Even though faith means the presence of Christ in a human being, and therefore the beginning of real righteousness—which is and remains God's own righteousness even when it is *in* a Christian—Christians cannot become sinless in this life.

The comfort of the continuous existence of the "flesh"

From the point of view of the fight between the "flesh" and the Spirit, no Christian can achieve sinlessness in this life. Luther holds that this is, in fact, a "greatest comfort." Namely, no Christian should be surprised by the power that the flesh still has over him or her:

> No one should be surprised or frightened when he feels this conflict of the flesh against the Spirit in his body, but he should fortify himself with these words of Paul: "The desires of the flesh are against the Spirit" and "These are opposed to each other, to prevent you from doing what you would." With these statements he is comforting those who are undergoing trials, as though he were saying: "It is impossible for you to follow the Spirit as your guide through everything without some awareness of hindrance by the flesh. Your flesh will be an obstacle, the sort of obstacle that

will prevent you from doing what you would. Here it is sufficient
if you resist the flesh and do not fulfill its desires, that is, if you
follow the Spirit rather than the flesh, which is easily disturbed
by impatience, which seeks revenge, grumbles, hates, bites back,
etc." When someone becomes aware of this battle of the flesh, he
should not lose heart on this account; but by the Spirit he should
fight back and say: "I am a sinner, and I am aware of my sin; for
I have not yet put off my flesh, to which sin will cling as long as
it lives. But I will obey the Spirit rather than the flesh. That is, by
faith and hope I will take hold of Christ. I will fortify myself with
His Word, and thus fortified I will refuse to fulfill the desires of
the flesh."[8]

Luther emphasizes that sin is such an integral part of the flesh
that any effort to destroy sin would lead to the destruction of the
flesh as well. Therefore, Christians do not need to rid themselves
of their "flesh" totally. They are "allowed" to feel the "desires of the
flesh," such as sadness, anxiety, anger, and so forth. Luther says:

> This passage provides us with the greatest possible comfort when
> it tells us that it is impossible to live without any desires and
> temptations of the flesh, in fact, without sin. It admonishes us
> not to act like the men of whom Gerson writes, who labored to
> rid themselves of any awareness of temptation or sin, in other
> words, to become nothing but stones. The sophists and monks
> had the notion about the saints that they were merely logs and
> blocks, utterly lacking in any feeling. Surely Mary felt a great sor-
> row in her mind when her Son was lost (Luke 2:48). Throughout
> the Psalms David complains that he is being almost swallowed up
> by the great sorrow that came from the magnitude of his tempta-
> tions and sins. Paul also complains that he feels "fighting without
> and fear within" (2 Cor. 7:5), and that with his flesh he serves
> the law of sin (Rom. 7:25). He says that he suffers "anxiety for all
> the churches" (2 Cor. 11:28), and that God had mercy on him by
> restoring Epaphroditus to life when he was near to death, lest he
> should have sorrow upon sorrow (Phil. 2:25-27). And so the saint
> as defined by the sophists resembles the wise man as defined by
> the Stoics.[9]

To "feel" vs. to "fulfill" the desires of the flesh

Sin in reality exists also in believers, working in them powerfully. For Luther, however, the acknowledgment of this fact does not mean that sin will be allowed to reign unchallenged. At this point, the significance of the notion of the presence of Christ in faith comes to the fore once again. Namely, it is essential to Christian life that sin is resisted with the help and the power of the Spirit of Christ. This resistance means that Christians do not "fulfill" the desires of the flesh. They are allowed to feel desire, but they must not give in to it. Believers may become angry, for example, but they must not harm other people in their anger. Luther says:

> When Paul says that the desires of the flesh are against the Spirit, etc., he impresses upon us at the same time that we are to be conscious of the desires of the flesh—not only of sensual desire, that is, but of pride, anger, sadness, impatience, unbelief, etc. But he wants us to be conscious of them in such a way that we do not give in to them or gratify them, that is, that we do not say and do what our flesh impels us to do. Thus when it impels us to anger, we should, as Ps. 4:4 teaches, "be angry" in such a way that we "sin not." It is as though Paul wanted to say: "I know that your flesh impels you to anger, envy, doubt, unbelief, and the like. But resist it by the Spirit, so that you do not sin. But if you forsake the guidance of the Spirit and follow the flesh, you will fulfill the desires of the flesh, and you will die" (Rom. 8:13).[10]

In Luther's point of view, sin no longer "reigns" in believers because the presence of the Spirit of Christ prevents the fulfilment of the desires of the flesh.

"Sin dominated by the Spirit of Christ" and the "dominating sin"

When Christ is present in faith, the "dominating sin" has been replaced by "the rule of the Spirit of Christ." The Reformer states:

Therefore let no one be so confident of himself as to suppose that when he has received grace, he is completely cleansed of his old vices. Many things are indeed cleansed, especially the head of the serpent—that is, unbelief and ignorance of God are cut off and crushed (Gen. 3:15)—but the scaly body and the remnants of sin still remain in us. Therefore let no one presume that once faith has been accepted, he can immediately undergo a metamorphosis into a new man. But he will still keep some of his old vices even in Christianity. For we are not dead yet; but we still live in the flesh, which, because it is not yet pure, has desires against the Spirit. . . . Therefore the natural vices that existed before faith remain also after faith has been accepted. But now they are being forced to serve the Spirit, who dominates them so that they do not rule; yet this does not happen without a struggle.[11]

When Luther discusses the nature of the "sin dominated by the Spirit of Christ," he presents—both in the quotation cited above and in many other passages—a view according to which all human beings have peculiar vices characteristic to them or vices related to their present life situations. All are troubled by their own painful and characteristic sins: some by the sins of carnal desires, others by the sin of hopelessness; some by the sin of greed, others by the sin of ambition. It is true that in faith these no longer dominate; however, they do not die, either, but are still there, smoldering.

Christians may become deeply troubled by their characteristic desires of the flesh, for example, by their bitterness, hatred, impatience, carnal lust, or melancholy. Moreover, the Reformer points out that even saints fall and "fulfill" the desires of the flesh. This happened to David, who became an adulterer and a murderer, and thus gave his opponents an occasion to blaspheme God. A similar thing happened to the "pillar" of the New Covenant, Peter, who denied Christ.

"Deliberate" and "unintended" falls

Luther emphasizes that saints, too, may fall and much more easily than might be expected. In fact, they even fall frequently. According to the Reformer, however, what makes a difference here is whether these falls occur "deliberately" or "out of weakness." Even if a saint falls often "because of weakness," he or she will not be denied forgiveness. However, if Christians fulfill the desires of the flesh "deliberately" and in a "carefree" manner, they are being deceitful and do not regard sin as sin anymore. The outcome of this, in turn, is that they no longer cry to Christ for mercy, and so they lose the Spirit of Christ and "die."[12]

The difference between a deliberate and an unintended fall is indicated very clearly in the following passage:

> They are not all of equal firmness of character, and many weaknesses and offenses are discernible in every one of them; it is also true that many of them fall into sin. But this does not hinder their holiness at all, so long as they sin out of weakness, not out of deliberate wickedness. For, as I have already said several times, the godly are conscious of the desires of the flesh; but they resist them and do not fulfill them. When they fall into sin unexpectedly, they obtain forgiveness, if by faith they return to Christ, who does not want us to chase away the lost sheep but to look for it. On no account, therefore, am I to jump to the conclusion that those who are weak in faith or morals are unholy, when I see that they love and revere the Word, receive the Lord's Supper, etc.; for God has received them and regards them as righteous through the forgiveness of sins. It is before Him that they stand or fall (Rom. 14:4).[13]

As indicated by this opposition of the deliberate and the unintended sin, it is crucial for the continuity and maintenance of faith and Christian life that in the middle of the fight against the flesh—and amid falls, too—one cries incessantly to Christ for mercy. At this point we can see, finally and clearly, who is the true subject, producer, and agent of sanctification: the Holy Spirit of Christ.

Chapter 9

The Sighing of the Spirit

The idea of the real presence of Christ is clearly manifested in Luther's view that in baptism the believer has fundamentally received the Holy Spirit, who is the Spirit of Christ. At this point, the "realistic" (ontological) way of thinking makes itself evident with particular clarity. On the one hand, the Reformer thinks that regarding the person of the Christian, the person of the Holy Spirit is in him or her as a kind of "other" reality. On the other hand, human beings cannot gain any knowledge of the presence of the Spirit (the "cry" of the Spirit) with their senses (*sensus*).[1]

According to Luther, the Spirit of Christ, who dwells in Christians, works in them by "helping" them in their weakness, which still exists in them. Thus, the help offered by the Spirit means that the Spirit "cries incessantly day and night" to Christ in Christians. As Luther says, "when we are, so to speak, so 'all-weak' (*omniinfirmi*) that we can scarcely emit a groan," the Spirit sighs in us "with sighs too deep for words." In the middle of the fight between the flesh and the Spirit, "in the midst of these terrors of the Law, thunderclaps of sin, tremors of death, and roarings of the devil, . . . the Holy Spirit begins to cry in our heart: 'Abba! Father!'"[2] Thus, when desperate human beings have no more strength to call on the merciful God (the "Father"), it is the Holy Spirit who "helps them in their weakness," intercedes (*interpellit*) for them "with sighs too deep for words," and bears witness before the spirit of each Christian that they are children of God.[3]

The aim of the sighs of the Spirit is to encourage human beings themselves to sigh and cry to God. The Spirit encourages Christians to take hold of the "word." Christians cannot hear the cries of the spirit; they only have the word (*verbum solum habemus*). When embracing this external word (God's promise), Christians themselves begin to sigh, too:

We have only the Word. If we take hold of this in the struggle, we breathe a little and sigh. To some extent we are aware of this sigh, but we do not hear the cry.[4]

Luther stresses that God hears the cries of the Spirit even though human beings do not know that through their senses. God, "He who searches the hearts of [people]," sees that this "infirm sigh" is a "loud cry," in comparison with which, as the Reformer continues,

> the great and horrible roars of the Law, sin, death, the devil, and hell are nothing at all and are inaudible. It is not without purpose, then, that Paul calls this sigh of the pious and afflicted heart the crying and indescribable sighing of the Spirit; for it fills all of heaven and cries so loudly that the angels suppose that they cannot hear anything except this cry.[5]

Human beings, in turn, appraise the cry of the Spirit quite differently:

> Within ourselves, however, there is the very opposite feeling. This faint sigh of ours does not seem to penetrate the clouds in such a way that it is the only thing to be heard by God and the angels in heaven. In fact, we suppose, especially as long as the trial continues, that the devil is roaring at us terribly, that heaven is bellowing, that the earth is quaking, that everything is about to collapse, that all the creatures are threatening us with evil, and that hell is opening up in order to swallow us. This feeling is in our hearts; we hear these terrible voices and see this frightening face. And this is what Paul says in 2 Cor. 12:9: that the power of Christ is made perfect in our weakness. For then Christ is truly almighty, and then He truly reigns and triumphs in us when we are, so to speak, so "all-weak" that we can scarcely emit a groan. But Paul says that in the ears of God this sigh is a mighty cry that fills all of heaven and earth.[6]

Luther points out that precisely the continuous and incessant sighs of the Spirit in the Christian are the "cannon" and the "instruments of war" with the help of which the plans of the enemy will be overcome in the course of time. The Reformer gives expression to this idea in a description that relates closely to his own life situation:

> Likewise in Luke 18:1-8, in the parable of the unjust judge, Christ calls this sigh of the pious heart a cry, and a cry that cries to God incessantly day and night. He says: "Hear what the unrighteous judge says. And will not God vindicate His elect, who cry to Him day and night? Will He delay long over them? I tell you, He will vindicate them speedily." Today, amid all the persecution and opposition from the pope, the tyrants, and the fanatical spirits, who attack us from the right and from the left, we cannot do anything but emit such sighs. But these have been our cannon and our instruments of war; with them we have frustrated the plans of our opponents all these years, and we have begun to demolish the kingdom of Antichrist.[7]

It is worth noting that the Holy Spirit cries "incessantly day and night" in the believer. Hence, it is not in fact Christians themselves who are sighing, but "it is sighed" in them, so to speak. It is obvious that Luther regards the Spirit as a distinct subject or agent in the believer. Consequently, the Spirit "cries" in Christians even when they are so desperate that they have no strength at all to cry to God themselves. Luther elucidates this, for example, in the following:

> Thus in Exodus the Lord says to Moses at the Red Sea (14:15): "Why do you cry to Me?" That was the last thing Moses was doing. He was in extreme anguish; therefore he was trembling and at the point of despair. Not faith but unbelief appeared to be ruling in him. For Israel was so hemmed in by the mountains, by the army of the Egyptians, and by the sea that it could not escape anywhere. Moses did not even dare mumble here. How, then, did he cry? Therefore we must not judge according to the feeling of our heart; we must judge according to the Word of God, which teaches that the Holy Spirit is granted to the afflicted, the terrified, and the despairing in such a way that He encourages and

comforts them, so that they do not succumb in their trials and other evils but conquer them, though not without very great fear and effort.[8]

There is no doubt about the fact that Luther considers the "sighing of the Spirit" as "another reality" in God's people: Moses did not cry to God at all, but God discerned the sigh of the Spirit in Moses' heart and heard it as a powerful cry. The same idea can be seen very clearly also in the following passage, in which the real and ontological nature of the presence of the Spirit is given explicit expression: the Holy Spirit was in the heart of Moses, not only "speculatively" but "really" (*non fuit speculative in Mose, sed re vera*). Luther even says that the Spirit "intercedes for Moses" with sighs too deep for words (*pro ipso interpellavit gemitu inenarrabili*). Luther undoubtedly also expresses his own *Anfechtung* in his call as a Reformer when he says:

> Thus I have just said that Moses saw the very presence of death in the water and wherever he turned his gaze. Therefore he was in the deepest anxiety and despair, and undoubtedly he sensed in his heart the loud cry of the devil against him, saying: "This entire people will perish today, for they cannot escape anywhere. You alone are responsible for this great calamity, for you led them out of Egypt." Then there came the cry of the people, who said (Ex. 14:11-12): "Is it because there are no graves in Egypt that you have taken us away to die in the wilderness? It would have been better for us to serve the Egyptians than to die in the wilderness." Then the Holy Spirit was present in Moses, not speculatively but actually [*re vera*]; He interceded for him with sighs too deep for words, so that Moses sighed to God and said: "Lord, it was at Thy command that I led the people out. Therefore do Thou help!" This sigh is what He calls "crying."[9]

Hence, the sighing of the Spirit happens in God's people as a kind of independent act, the true agent and subject being the Spirit of Christ. In this way, the Spirit and the Spirit's incessant sighs guarantee that the Christian's struggle continues. The essential points here are, firstly, that the work of the Spirit is always connected with the word, and, secondly, that the aim of the sighing of the Spirit is that a troubled human being can "take hold of the word" and appropriate it.

Chapter 10

Realistic Symbolism and the Union with Christ

The word as a "womb"

Luther says that, owing to the fact that the cry of the Spirit cannot be discerned with the human senses, "we have only the word" (*verbum solum habemus*). When Christians grasp the word, they find some comfort in the midst of their despair, and so they begin to "sigh to God" themselves, too. Luther states that when believers themselves—and not only the Holy Spirit—begin to sigh, they already have "this faint sigh and this tiny faith, which depends only on hearing the sound of the voice of Christ as He promises."[1] However, their sighing, which has thus begun, does not cry "eloquently" or "tearfully." Their sighing is only about a "word," but this word contains "everything."[2]

From the point of view of the knowledge gained by the human senses (*quoad sensum*), the word of promise seems like a tiny and insignificant "center point." In reality, however, the word is like an "arch of immeasurable width" curving over God and all God's treasures. Therefore a human being, when taking hold of the word of God, becomes a partaker of the "divine life" itself. Luther says, for example: "Through the spoken Word we receive fire and light, by which we are made new and different, and by which a new judgment, new sensations, and new drives arise in us."[3]

Hence, according to Luther, it is the word and not the human being that is the active agent. The word gives birth to the Christian, and this is *God's* work in him or her. Thus, this view of Luther also reveals that the Reformer's theology of the word is internally related to his doctrine of justification. Luther speaks of the passive nature of the Christian's birth that happens with the word in this way:

Paul calls the church barren because her children are not born by means of the Law or works or any human efforts of powers but in the Holy Spirit through the Word of faith. This is purely a matter of being born, not of doing any works. Those who are prolific, on the other hand, labor and strain greatly in travail; this is purely a matter of doing works, not of giving birth.[4]

Because the "word" gives birth to a new human being, Luther likens it to a womb, in which the believer is conceived and carried; this reflects the Reformer's realistic way of thinking.

Whoever is a son must be an heir as well. For merely by being born he deserves to be an heir. No work and no merit brings him the inheritance, but only his birth. Thus he obtains the inheritance in a purely passive, not in an active way; that is, just his being born, not his producing or working or worrying, makes him an heir. He does not do anything toward his being born but merely lets it happen. Therefore we come to these eternal goods—the forgiveness of sins, righteousness, the glory of the resurrection, and eternal life—not actively but passively. Nothing whatever interferes here; faith alone takes hold of the offered promise. Therefore just as in society a son becomes an heir merely by being born, so here faith alone makes [people] sons [and daughters] of God, born of the Word, which is the divine womb in which we are conceived, carried, born, reared, etc. By this birth and this patience or passivity which makes us Christians we also become sons [and daughters] and heirs. But being heirs, we are free of death and the devil, and we have righteousness and eternal life.[5]

The church as "mother"

Just as Luther likens the word to a womb in a manner that is, in fact, almost "physically" realistic, he also calls the church a mother who gives birth to her children, that is, Christians. It is the church that brings Christians to "perfection," to the likeness of the form of Christ, until they come of age. The Reformer says:

Therefore just as Isaac has the inheritance from his father solely on the basis of the promise and of his birth, without the Law or works, so we are born as heirs by Sarah, the free woman, that is, by the church. She teaches, cherishes, and carries us in her womb, her bosom, and her arms; she shapes and perfects us to the form of Christ, until we grow into perfect manhood (Eph 4:13). Thus everything happens through the ministry of the Word.[6]

The ministry of the word as "father"

According to Luther, the church as mother "gives birth" by means of the ministry of the church, as the passage quoted above shows. The church carries her children when practicing the ministry of the word:

Therefore Sarah, or Jerusalem, our free mother, is the church, the bride of Christ who gives birth to all. She goes on giving birth to children without interruption until the end of the world, as long as she exercises the ministry of the Word, that is, as long as she preaches and plants the Gospel; for this is what it means for her to give birth.[7]

Just as Luther speaks of the word as a womb and of the church as mother, using physical-natural imagery, so he also speaks of the apostles and those practicing the ministry of the word as "fathers" who "give birth to the form of the soul".[8]

"With whom I am again in travail." This is an allegory. The apostles—like all teachers, though in a special way—acted in the place of parents; just as the latter give birth to the form of the body, so the former to the form of the mind. Now the form of the Christian mind is faith, the trust of the heart, which takes hold of Christ, clings only to Him [lecture notes: *inhereat ei*] and to nothing else besides. A heart that is equipped with such confidence has the true form of Christ, which is provided by the ministry of the word. . . . For the Word proceeds from the mouth of the apostle and reaches the heart of the hearer; there the Holy

Spirit is present and impresses that Word on the heart, so that it is heard. In this way every preacher is a parent [lecture notes: *artifex*; Erlangen Edition: *pater*], who produces and forms the true shape of the Christian mind through the ministry of the Word.[9]

The means of grace committed to the church, that is, the word of God and the sacraments, are decisive in the Christian's struggle. These means are the true source of the holiness of Christians.

Chapter 11

The Present Christ and the Objective Basis for Holiness

Means of grace as "essential signs" (central signs of the essence)

The Reformer interprets the means of grace with the help of a particular theory of signs, according to which the word and the sacraments are "essential signs."[1] This means that in these signs, contrary to other signs, the essence of the representation and the essence of what is being represented are identical. The essence of the representation *is* the essence of what is being represented. Therefore, in receiving God's word and a sacrament, one always receives the whole essence of God, too. God's saving activity always takes place through an external sign, but at the same time in a manner that involves the human being's essential relationship with God.

Luther's theory of signs is one factor that helps us to understand how a human being becomes "holy," that is, how he or she is "created after the likeness of God."[2] According to Luther, the likeness of the image of Christ (*imago Dei*) means that God's people understand and know in the same way as Christ does; that is, they understand and know Christ himself. The Reformer says (according to his lecture notes):

> The image of God or Christ: that is, to perceive, feel, want, understand, and think as Christ—or, to perceive (etc.) Christ himself. It is, namely, the will and spirit of Christ that he died for our sins, in obedience to the Father. To believe this is to be made in the image of Christ. This is "the new [person], created" etc.[3]

Thus, one is born in the image of God, born a new human being, that is, born holy, by believing that God has, out of sheer love, taken the place of human beings and carried their sins. By looking at this "representation" of Christ, the Christian receives the same form that Christ has (*habeant eandem formam in animo quam Deus vel Christus*).[4] As this indicates, the word of Christ is an "essential sign" that transmits its likeness to the believer. Hence, the objectivity of the means of grace—an aspect emphasized by Luther—does not imply abandonment of the notion of the presence of Christ in faith.

Holiness and the distinctive religious way of life

To repeat, the holiness of Christians is totally based on "external signs," that is, on the word and the sacraments. This implies, first of all, that believers are *not* made holy by their withdrawal from the "world," or by their adoption of a particularly religious way of life. Hence, the sanctity of Christians is not based on their being different from the world because of their more ascetic way of life. Luther's appraisal of this kind of lifestyle is very critical:

> The world admires the holiness of Benedict, Gregory, Bernard, Francis, and men like that, because it hears that they performed works that looked magnificent and unusual. Surely St. Ambrose, Augustine, and others were saints also. They did not live such an ascetic and horrible life as these others but remained in human society, eating ordinary food, drinking wine, and wearing fine, decent clothing. So far as the ordinary customs of life were concerned, there was almost no difference between them and other respectable men; and yet they deserve to be preeminent over the ones mentioned earlier. For without any superstition they taught the faith of Christ in its purity, battled against heretics, and purified the church of innumerable errors. Their company brought joy to many, and especially to the sorrowful and the distressed, whom they encouraged and comforted with the Word; for they did not withdraw from human society but carried out their responsibilities amid frequent disturbances. Those others, by contrast, not only taught many things that were contrary to the faith but were also the originators of many superstitions, errors, and ungodly forms of worship. Therefore unless they took hold

of Christ in the hour of death and trusted solely in His death and victory, their ascetic life was of no use to them at all.[5]

Holiness and heresies

Secondly, because it is the external signs, the means of grace that make one holy, Christians' holiness is also not based on their ability to avoid heresies in life or in doctrine. By contrast, it is very interesting that the continuing existence of the desires of the flesh in Christians does actually result in doctrinal errors. Indeed, Luther points out that because "the old Adam [and Eve]" is still alive, the heresies into which saints fall are not only "minor" doctrinal misdemeanors but sometimes even "dangerous doctrinal errors." Luther offers three exaples: Gregory was the originator of the Low Mass, monks invented self-chosen acts of religious devotion, and Cyprian insisted that the baptism of those who had been baptized by heretics was invalid. According to Luther, however, God does not hold these errors against these Christians, because they took refuge in Christ in their struggle against the flesh, and because God imputed this faith to them as righteousness.[6]

The hidden holiness of the church

Thus, even though Luther considers the church holy, he does not regard it as totally free from sin and doctrinal errors. The Reformer says that God "conceals and covers [the church's holiness] with weaknesses, sins, errors, and various offenses and forms of the cross."[7] Therefore, the natural knowing capacity of human beings can never discern God's sanctifying activity in the church. Only the eye of faith can see what God does in the church in order to sanctify human beings. Therefore (in spite of the fact that the church is something that can be observed empirically, rather than being a Platonic idea), it is vital that in the article of the Creed, "I believe in a holy church," "I believe" is not replaced by "I see."[8] Namely, what would happen in the latter case is that one would begin to seek the source of holiness in human beings and their works, instead of seeking it in Christ, who is the true source of holiness. True holiness is a "righteousness given as a gift," in which human beings are freed from the obligation to perform works in order to achieve salvation; thus, they can direct their activities to the service of their neighbors. Holiness means that in the middle of the conflict between the flesh and the Spirit Christians turn again and again—with the strength given to them by the Spirit and in prayer for forgiveness—to the objective reality that is outside them and makes them holy. This reality is Christ himself, the favor and the gift of God. He is the objective but at the same time also the subjective basis for holiness: "*Sic ut Christus sit obiectum fidei, imo non obiectum, sed, ut ita dicam, in ipsa fide Christus adest.*"[9]

Conclusion

The aim of this study was to find out whether the Lutheran understanding of Christian faith includes a theological motif analogous to the doctrine of divinization, a central notion in the Orthodox interpretation of Christian faith.

Luther's commentary on Paul's Epistle to the Galatians (*Lectures on Galatians,* 1531, 1535) was chosen as the main source for this study. This commentary, as stated in one of the Lutheran confessional texts, the *Formula of Concord,* contains the fundamental presentation of the Lutheran doctrine of justification.

The analysis of Luther's theology in his *Lectures on Galatians* shows that his doctrine of justification involves a way of thinking that can be described by using the technical term "divinization" or "deification." The idea of divinization is present in Luther's theology not only as a term but also in content.

Luther's idea of divinization finds succinct expression in his well-known sentence: *in ipsa fide Christus adest.*

Unlike the *Formula of Concord* and later Lutheran theology, Luther does not separate justification and the presence of Christ in the believer. According to Luther, Christ is, in one and the same person, *both* God's "favor" (forgiveness, the removal of God's wrath, and the "justification" of which the *Formula of Concord* speaks) *and* God's "gift" (God's presence in God's very being, and human "participation in the divine nature"; 2 Peter 1:4).

According to Luther, justification is not merely a new ethical or juridical relation between God and a human being. When a human being believes in Christ, Christ is present, in the very fullness of his divine and human nature, in that faith itself. Luther understands the presence of Christ in such a concrete way that, according to his view, Christ and the Christian become "one person." In this "happy exchange," the human being becomes a partaker of God's attributes. The attributes that Luther mentions most often are "life," "righteousness," "wisdom," "salvation" ("blessedness"), "power," "joy," "courage," "new understanding," and "love."

The idea of Christ's real presence in faith sheds light on the meaning of many of those themes in Luther's theology that have continued to be subjects of controversy among scholars up to the present day. This idea makes apprehensible the Reformer's understanding of the relationships between justification and sanctification, real and declarative righteousness, and the partial and total aspects of the idea of "simultaneously righteous and a sinner." At the same time, the idea of the presence of Christ offers a perspective for understanding Luther's view of the continuity of the Christian existence, which, according to the Reformer, rests on the "incessant sighs of the Spirit." This hidden spiritual life is truly "happening" and effective in believers, even though they cannot always perceive it in themselves.

The notion of the real presence of Christ in faith supposes a strong subjective or existential aspect in Luther's thinking. This notion, however, is not in conflict with the Lutheran position on the centrality of the word and sacraments and their pivotal role in the Lutheran doctrine of justification. The source of "Christian holiness" is in the "external signs" of the means of grace, which, as "essential signs," are the agents of righteousness and of one's essential, ontological relationship with God.

In spite of the fact that Luther's theology includes a specific and clear idea of divinization, one must not automatically identify this concept in Luther's use with the patristic-Orthodox concept of divinization. Within the framework of this study, in accordance with its aim, it has only been possible to conclude that Luther's theology has a notion analogous to the Orthodox doctrine of *theopoesis*, and, furthermore, that this notion is central to the Reformer's doctrine of justification as well as to his entire theology. A comparison between the Orthodox and the Lutheran concepts of divinization is, undoubtedly, one of the promising research tasks that lie ahead.

Notes

Editor's Introduction

1. This introduction concentrates on the work of Tuomo Mannermaa. However, the reader should keep in mind that "the Finnish Luther Research" today consists of several perspectives developed by a number of Luther scholars who have been engaged in intensive, often collaborative work on Luther. Many results of this work have been published in multi-author volumes (see the bibliography). As Risto Saarinen, one of the leading scholars in this "school," says on his website, the "'Mannermaa school' is by no means putting forward a monolithic interpretation of the German Reformer or claiming that we can today compile a Lutheran Summa theologiae. Over-simplifications . . . should also be avoided." He names several trends and main interests in this Finnish research: the real presence of Christ in the believer, theology of love and theology of the cross, sacraments and ecclesiology, and issues related to ontology. He also notes that although most of this work is done within the discipline of systematic theology, it also makes historical claims. See www.helsinki.fi/~risaarin/luther.html for an overview and list of sources.

2. Simo Peura explicates the idea of indwelling to mean that "a Christian is a god, God's child and infinite, because God indwells in him [or her]" (WA 4:280, 2-5). In other words, "Deification means for the Christian participation in God and in his divine nature" (WA 3:106, 14-15). Simo Peura, "Christ as Favor and Gift: The Challenge of Luther's Understanding of Justification," in *Union with Christ: The New Finnish Interpretation of Luther*, ed. Carl E. Braaten and Robert W. Jenson (Grand Rapids: Eerdmans, 1998), 51.

3. Tuomo Mannermaa, "Why Is Luther So Fascinating?" in Braaten and Jenson, *Union with Christ*, 10.

4. Ibid., 12.

5. Ibid., 6.

6. On ecumenical implications, see, e.g., Risto Saarinen's "Salvation in the Lutheran-Orthodox Dialogue," in Braaten and Jenson, *Union with Christ*, 167–81.

7. Scott Hendrix, "Martin Luther's Reformation of Spirituality," *Lutheran Quarterly* 13/3 (Autumn 1999), 258. See Kirsi Stjerna, "Luther, Lutherans and Spirituality," in *Spirituality: Toward a 21st Century Lutheran Understanding*, ed. K. Stjerna and B. Schramm (Minneapolis: Lutheran University Press, 2004), for reflections on how the Finnish Luther interpretation offers a way to appreciate the potential and uniqueness of Luther's and Lutheran spirituality.

8. Braaten and Jenson, "Preface: The Finnish Breakthrough in Luther Research," *Union with Christ*, viii.

9. Risto Saarinen in his website introduction to the Finnish Luther studies states that the "Finnish approach is often very critical of earlier research paradigms. We claim that the post-Enlightenment Luther research has been seriously burdened by confessional and philosophical pre-conditions, among which the overall hostility to 'ontological' issues is one of the most important ones." See www.helsinki.fi/~risaarin/luther.html, "Overview."

10. Mannermaa himself has written two articles in English that provide a marvelous and succinct introduction to and summary of his interpretation of Luther. These articles, titled "Why Is Luther So Fascinating?" and "Justification and Theosis in Lutheran-Orthodox Perspective," can both be found in Braaten and Jenson, *Union with Christ*, 1–20, 25–41. Also essential reading are Simo Peura's articles in the same volume, "Christ as Favor and Gift; The Challenge of Luther's Understanding of Justification" (42–68) and "What God Gives Man Receives: Luther on Salvation" (76–95). In the same work, Sammeli Juntunen and Antti Raunio offer important articles on Luther's notion of "being" and the ethics of the Golden Rule in Luther's theology. See, respectively, "Luther and Metaphysics: What Is the Structure of Being according to Luther?" (129–60) and "Natural Law and Faith: The Forgotten Foundations of Luther's Theology" (96–124).

11. Juhani Forsberg's dissertation, *Das Abrahambild in der Theologie Luthers: Pater fidei sanctissimus* (Stuttgart, 1984), already laid out the main principles and perspectives of the new Finnish Luther study that followed. Risto Saarinen's dissertation *Gottes Wirken auf uns: Die transzendentale Deutung des Gegenwart-Christi-Motivs in der Lutherforschung*

(Wiesbaden, 1989) and Simo Peura's dissertation *Mehr als ein Mensch: Die Vergöttlichung als Thema der Theologie Martin Luthers von 1513- bis 1519* (Mainz, 1994) followed. Saarinen examines those theological and philosophical elements that led to the schools of thought that left the idea of the participation of Christ and the *theosis* motif in the background in Luther research. Peura studies the role of the *theosis* motif in Luther's theology as a whole. Antti Raunio's *Summe des christlichen Lebens: Die 'Goldene Regel' als Gesetz der Liebe in der Theologie Martin Luthers von 1510–1527* (Mainz, 2001) looks at Luther's theology as simultaneously totally a theology of faith and totally a theology of love. Sammeli Juntunen's *Der Begriff des Nichts bei Luther in den Jahren von 1510 bis 1523* (Helsinki, 1996) analyzes the reformer's use of the concepts "Nichts" and "nihil" in relation to their polar opposite, "being" ("sein," "esse"). Pekka Kärkkäinen's dissertation on *Luthers trinitarische Theologie des Heiligen Geistes* (Helsinki, 2003) focuses on Luther's doctrine of the Trinity and pneumatology.

Introduction

1. On Luther's relation to mysticism, see Erich Vogelsang, "Luther und die Mystik," *Luther-Jahrbuch* XIX (Berlin, 1937), 32–54. [Also valuable is Bengt Hoffman's work, *Theology of the Heart: The Role of Mysticism in the Theology of Martin Luther* (Minneapolis: Kirk House, 1998).—Ed.]

2. For a criticism of the "physical" interpretation see, e.g., Arnold Gilg, *Der Weg und Bedeutung der altkirchlichen Christologie* (Munich: Chr. Kaiser, 1955); Werner Elert, *Der Ausgang der altkirchlichen Christologie* (Berlin: Lutherisches Verlagshaus, 1957).

3. Dietrich Ritschl, *Athanasius: Versuch einer Interpretation* (Theologische Studien 76; Zürich: EVZ Verlag, 1964).

4. Ibid.

5. "Accordingly we reject and condemn all the following errors: . . . 6. That not God himself but only divine gifts dwell in believers." *The Book of Concord: The Confessions of the Evangelical Lutheran Church*, trans. and ed. Theodore G. Tappert (Philadelphia: Muhlenberg, 1959), 474–75. [The preferred edition today is the 2000 translation of the *Book of Concord*, edited by Timothy Wengert and Robert Kolb (Minneapolis: Fortress).— Ed.] "Repudiamus ergo et damnamus omnia falsa dogmata, quae iam recitabimus: . . . VI. Non ipsum Deum, sed tantum dona Dei in credentibus habitare." *Die Bekenntnisschriften der evangelisch-lutherischen Kirche* (Göttingen: Vandenhoeck & Ruprecht, 1986), 785.

6. Tappert, *The Book of Concord*, 548–49; *Bekenntnisschriften*, 932–33.

7. *Lectures on Galatians* (1535), *LW* 26–27:149; *In epistolam S. Pauli ad Galatas Commentarius ex praelectione D. Martini Lutheri collectus* (1531) 1535, WA 40/1–40/2:184.

On Luther's *Lectures on Galatians* see Bornkamm, Karin, *Luthers Auslegungen des Galaterbriefs von 1519 und 1531. Ein Vergleich* (Arbeiten zur Kirchengeschichte, 35; Berlin, 1963).

8. "Was dann ferner zu eigentlicher Erklärung dieses hohen und vornehmen Artikels der Rechtfertigung für Gott vonnöten, daran unser Seelen Seligkeit gelegen, wollen wir männiglich auf die schöne und herrliche Auslegung D. Luthers über die Epistel S. Pauli an die Galater gewiesen und umb geliebter Kürze hiermit gezogen haben." The Latin version reads: "Quod praeterea ad copiosiorem huius ardui et praecipui articuli iustificationis coram Deo (in quo nostra salus vertitur) explicationem requiritur, de eo praeclarum D. Lutheri commentarium in epistolam Pauli ad Galatas ab unoquoque consuli et diligenter legi monemus, ad quem brevitatis studio hoc loco nos referimus." *Bekenntnisschriften*, 936. The English translation by Tappert reads as follows: "If anybody regards anything more as necessary by way of a detailed explanation of this high and important article of justification before God, on which the salvation of our souls depends, we direct him for the sake of brevity to Dr. Luther's beautiful and splendid exposition of St. Paul's Epistle to the Galatians." *The Book of Concord*, 551.

9. In some cases references will also be made to other works of Luther, if they essentially clarify the subject in question.

10. "Diese Einsicht spricht sich m. E. in der auf patristischer Grundlage fußenden, orthodoxen Lehre von der Theopoiesis des Menschen aus. Diese Lehre, die von protestantischer Seite so oft verdächtigt worden ist, gibt derselben Intention Ausdruck wie die evangelische Lehre von der Rechtfertigung allein durch den Glauben: Nur durch Gott selbst, d. h. durch den Heiligen Geist, kann der Mensch an Gott glauben und Gott lieben und dadurch gerecht werden. Gott in Christus ist selbst des Menschen Gerechtigkeit vor ihm. Das schließt aber ein, daß der im Glauben gerechte Mensch in das sein Gottes hineingenommen wird." Regin Prenter, *Theologie und Gottesdienst: Gesammelte Aufsätze* (Arhus: Aros, 1977), 289, Anm. 10.

11. Georg Kretschmar, "Kreuz und Auferstehung in der Sicht von Athanasios und Luther" (S. 67, Anm. 60), in Kirchliches Außenamt der

EKD (Hrsg.): *Der auferstandene Christus und das Heil der Welt. Das Kirch-berger Gespräch über die Bedeutung der Auferstehung für das Heil der Welt zwischen Vertretern der Evangelischen Kirche in Deutschland und der Russischen Orthodoxen Kirche* (Studienheft 7, Witten, 1972), 40–82. I would like to mention here that discussions with Kretschmar have decisively encouraged me to write this study.

Über die anthropologischen Grenzen der Kirche by Konstantinos E. Papapetrou does not set out, in spite of the subtitle of the book (*Ein philosophisch-theologischer Entwurf zum Thema Simul iustus et peccator aus orthodox-katholischer Sicht* ["A philosophico-theological study on the theme 'Simul iustus et peccator' from the Orthodox-Catholic point of view"]), to search for a point of contact between the doctrine of divinization and that of justification (*Arbeiten zur Geschichte und Theologie des Luthertums*, Bd. 26, Hamburg: Lutherisches Verlagshaus, 1972).

12. See, e.g., Heinrich Bornkamm, *Luther, Gestalt und Wirkungen: Gesammelte Aufsätze* (Gütersloh: G. Mohn, 1975), and "Zur Frage der iustitia Dei beim jungen Luther," *Archiv für Reformationsgeschichte* 52 (1961) 15–19 and 53 (1962) 1–59. A work by Emanuel Hirsch, *Die Theologie des Andreas Osiander und ihre geschichtlichen Voraussetzungen* (Göttingen: Vandenhoeck & Ruprecht, 1919) is of special significance for the present study. See also Hirsch's important article "Initium theologiae Lutheri," *Lutherstudien* II (Gütersloh: C. Bertelsmann, 1954) 9–35. See also Erich Seeberg, *Luthers Theologie* I–II (Göttingen: Vandenhoeck & Ruprecht, 1929; Stuttgart, 1937) and Erich Vogelsang, *Die Anfänge von Luthers Christologie nach der ersten Psalmenvorlesung* (Leipzig and Berlin: W. de Gruyter, 1929).

13. Wilhelm Maurer, "Die Einheit der Theologie Luthers," *Kirche und Geschichte: Gesammelte Aufsätze* (Göttingen: Vandenhoeck & Ruprecht, 1970), 1:11–21.

Ernst Wolf's critique of Maurer's thesis is based on dialectical theology. See Ernst Wolf, "Asterisci und Obelisci zum Thema: Athanasios und Luther," *Evangelische Theologie* 18 (1958) 481ff. Wolf sets against each other Luther's theology of the word and cross on one hand, and Athanasius's notion of the philanthropy of God on the other. It must be noted, however, that the theme of philanthropy is an essential motif in Luther's theology. The Luther quotations in the following are taken from the Erlangen Edition (Erlanger Ausgabe, EA) with slightly modernized German. "Er braucht hie nicht das Wörtlin Gnade, wie droben; sondern zwei liebliche ander Wort, Freundlichkeit und Leutseligkeit schreibet er dem gnädigen Gott zu. Das erste heiss auf Griechisch Chrestotes, und ist das freundlich, lieblich Wandeln eines gütigen Lebens, daß jedermann gerne mit demselbigen Menschen umbgehet, und sein Gesellschaft fast süß, jedermann zu Gunst und Liebe reizet, der die Leut wohl leiden kann, niemand veracht, niemand mit sauren, harten, seltzamen Geberden oder Weise verjagt, mag jedermann zuversichtlich umb ihn sein, zu ihm gehen und mit ihm handeln; gleichwie die Evangelia Christum abmalen unter den Leuten, der jedermann freundlich ist, niemand veracht, niemand versagt, und ganz schlachtig, mört und nietig ist." *Kirchenpostille* (1522), EA 2, 7, 165; WA 10/1:95–128. Cf. also the following passage, in which Luther speaks of the philanthropy of God explicitly: "Ich thar sagen, daß ich in der ganzen Schrift nicht lieblicher Wort habe gelesen von Gottes Gnaden geredt, denn diese zwei: Chrestotes und Philanthropia, darin die Gnade also abgemalet ist, daß sie nicht allein Sünde vergebe, sondern auch bei uns wohne, freundlich mit uns umbgehe, willig ist zu helfen, und urbietig zu thun alles, was wir begehrn mügen, als von einem guten willigen Freunde, zu dem sich ein Mensch alles Gutes versiehet und sich ganz wohl vermag. Erdenk dir also einen guten Freund, so hastu ein Bild, wie sich Gott gegen dir in Christo erbeut; und ist dennoch solchs Bild noch gar geringe, solche überreichte Gnade furzubilden." *Kirchenpostille* (1522), EA 2, 7, 169; WA 10/1:95–128.

The presuppositions of dialectical theology make Wolf interpret Luther one-sidedly. Luther carries the idea of the philanthropy of God so far that he likens God to a "dog, horse and dolphin," which "have a natural desire and love for man." "Das ander heißet Philanthropia, Menschenlieb; gleichwie Geiz möcht Geldliebe heissen. Und David 2. Regum (V. 26) Frauenbegierd nennen Frauenliebe. Also nennen die natürlichen Meister etliche Thiere Menschenlieber oder leutselig; als da sind die Hund, Pferd, Delphin. Denn dieselbigen Thier haben natürlich Lust und Liebe zu den Menschen. Ein solchen Namen und Liebe eignet hie der Apostel unserm Gott, und hat zuvor auch gethan Moses Deuter. 33 (V. 2.3.), da er von Gott sagt: zu seiner rechten Hand ist ein feuriges Gesetz; wie hat er die Leute so lieb! Daß die Meinung sei: Gott hat sich im Evangelio nicht allein freundlich erzeiget, der jedermann um sich leiden und annehmen wölle; sondern wiederumb hält er sich auch zu ihnen, suchet bei ihnen zu sein, beut ihnen seine Gnade und Freundschaft an." *Kirchenpostille* (1522), EA 2, 7, 166; WA 10/1:98.

14. [The following explanation regarding this word choice is a paraphrased translation of an e-mail message where Mannermaa discusses the matter. Mannermaa approves of this word choice. In his earlier writings Mannermaa actually used the word "ontological" instead of "ontic." However, the term was often misunderstood to associate Luther with a nominalist philosophy, something which was not intended at all. The most common misunderstanding was that Mannermaa's use of the word "ontological" would suggest that Luther represents an Aristotelian type of "substance ontology." Mannermaa is not making that claim but rather maintains that Luther does not represent any particular established philosophical ontology. When he uses the term "esse" ("Sein," in German; "being" or "to be") when describing the way in which Christ is present in faith, he uses the term in a theological rather than philosophical sense. Because of the misunderstandings around the term "ontology," Mannermaa began to use the word "onttinen," which translates as "ontic" (or "reaali-onttinen," meaning "real ontic"). With this term he referred simply to "that which has to do with being" ("sein betreffend," "Seinschaft" in German), with no implication or intention of tying into or applying any broader ontological systems. In German scholarship the language has been much influenced by Martin Heidegger's language, where "ontic" is used about the "lower" part of the human reality, the concrete ("gegenständlich") reality; the concept "ontological," then, refers to the existential reality. The former can be characterized by the concept "to be" ("sein," in German), and the latter with the word "being" ("seiende" in German; "esse" in Latin). This being the case, the use of the word "ontic" only ended up reinforcing the misunderstanding that Finnish Luther research would represent a "concretizing," "substance ontological" view in a Heideggerian sense. For these reasons, Mannermaa has returned to using his original term, "ontological" ("ontologinen," in Finnish).—Ed.]

15. [The Finnish wording "kristityn kilvoittelu," which could be translated also as "fight of faith," describes the Pauline idea of the Christian's battle against sin and attempt to live a life of faith with the spirit.—Ed.]

Chapter 1: The Basis for Justifying Faith

1. *Lectures on Galatians* (1535), *LW* 26:277. "Et hoc viderunt omnes Prophetae, quod Christus futurus esset omnium maximus latro, homicida, adulter, fur, sacrilegus, blasphemus etc., quo nullus maior unquam in mundo fuerit. Quia iam non gerit personam suam. Iam non est natus

de virgine Dei filius, sed peccator, qui habet et portat peccatum Pauli qui fuit blasphemus, persecutor et violentus; Petri qui negavit Christum; Davidis qui fuit adulter, homicida et blasphemare fecit Gentes nomen Domini; In summa, qui habet et portat omnia omnium peccata in corpore suo. Non quod ipse commiserit ea, sed quod ea a nobis commissa susceperit in corpus suum, pro illis sanguine proprio satisfacturus." WA 40/1:433, 26–434, 12 (published text).

2. "Et sic comprehenditur ut aliquis, qui inter latrones, si etiam innocens. Quantomagis si sponte sua et patris voluntate voluit communicare corpus et sanguinem eorum, qui erant latrones, peccatores. Ideo submersus in omnia." *In epistolam S. Pauli ad Galatas Commentarius ex praelectione D. Martini Luther collectus* (1535). WA 40/1:434, 1-4 (lecture notes).

3. *Lectures on Galatians* (1535), *LW* 26:278. "Sed valde absurdum et contumeliosum est filium Dei appellare peccatorem et maledictum. Si vis negare eum esse peccatorem et maledictum, negato etiam passum, crucifixum et mortuum. Non enim minus absurdum est dicere filium Dei, ut fides nostra confitetur et orat, crucifixum, poenas peccati et mortis sustinuisse, quam peccatorem aut maledictum dicere. Si vero non est absurdum confiteri et credere Christum crucifixum inter Latrones, neque absurdum sit eum dicere meledictum et peccatorem peccatorum." . . . "Ad eundem modum loquitur et Esaias Ca. 53. de Christo, 'Deus' inquiens, 'posuit omnium nostrum iniquitates in Ipsum'. Ista vocabula non sunt extenuanda, sed sinenda esse propria et seria. Deus enim non iocatur verbis Prophetae, sed serio loquitur et ex magna charitate, Videlicet, quod ille Agnus Dei, Christus, debeat portare iniquitates omnium nostrum. At quid est portare? Respondent Sophistae: puniri. Bene. Sed quare Christus punitur? An non ideo, quia peccatum habet et gerit? Quod autem peccatum habeat Christus, testatur etiam Spiritus sanctus in Psalm. Ut Psalm. 39.: 'Comprehenderunt me iniquitates meae.' Et Psalm. 40.: 'Ego dixi: Domine, miserere mei, sana animam meam, quia peccavi tibi.' Et Psalm. 68: 'Deus, tu scis insipientiam meam et delicta mea a te non sunt abscondita.' In his Psalmis loquitur Spiritus sanctus in persona Christi et manifestis verbis testatur eum peccasse sive peccata habere. Sunt tamen haec testimonia Psalmorum voces non innocentis, sed patientis Christi qui personam omnium peccatorum gerendam suscepit ideoque reus factus est peccatorum totius mundi." WA 40/1:434, 29-36; 435, 21–436, 16 (published text).

4. *Lectures on Galatians* (1535), *LW* 26:280. "Ista est iucundissima omnium doctrinarum et consolationis plenissima quae docet habere

nos hanc ineffabilem et inaestimabilem misericordiam et charitatem Dei, scilicet: cum videret misericors Pater per legem nos opprimi et sub maledicto teneri nec ulla re nos posse ab eo liberari, quod miserit in mundum filium suum in quem omnia omnium peccata coniecit et dixit ad eum: Tu sis Petrus ille negator, Paulus ille persecutor, blasphemus et violentus, David ille adulter, peccator ille qui comedit pomum in Paradiso, Latro ille in Cruce, In Summa, tu sis omnium hominum persona qui feceris omnium hominum peccata, tu ergo cogita, ut solvas et pro eis satisfacias." WA 40/1:437, 18-27 (published text). Compare this quote with Luther's hymn "Dear Christians, Let Us Now Rejoice," *LW* 53:219–20 ("Nun freut euch, lieben Christen gmein," WA 35:422–25; *Evangelisches Kirchengesangbuch* 239).

5. *Lectures on Galatians* (1535), *LW* 26:282. ". . . *divina virtus, iustitia, benedictio, gratia et vita.*" WA 40/1:440, 21.

6. *Lectures on Galatians* (1535), *LW* 26:282. WA 40/1:26–30.

7. *Lectures on Galatians* (1535), *LW* 26:282. "Quatenus igitur Christus per gratiam suam in cordibus fidelium regnat, nullum peccatum, mors, maledictio est. Ubi vero Christus non cognoscitur, manent ista. Ideo carent isto beneficio et victoria omnes, qui non credunt. 'Est enim victoria nostra', ut Iohannes ait, 'fides.'" WA 40/1:440, 31-35.

8. *Lectures on Galatians* (1535), *LW* 26:282. WA 40/1:441, 19-28.

9. *Lectures on Romans* (1515–1516), *LW* 25:332. WA 56:343, 16-21.

10. *Lectures on Galatians* (1535), *LW* 26:285–86. "Quod autem Christo nunc regnante nullum re vera amplius Peccatum, Mors et Maledictio sit, confitemur etiam quotidie in Symbolo Apostolorum, cum dicimus: 'Credo Ecclesiam sanctam:' Quod plane nihil aliud est, quam si diceremus: Credo nullum peccatum, nullam mortem in Ecclesia esse; Quia credentes in Christum non sunt peccatores, non sunt rei mortis, sed simpliciter sancti et iusti, domini peccati et mortis et in aeternum viventes. Verum hoc tantum fides cernit, quia dicimus: 'Credo Ecclesiam sanctam.' Si autem rationem et oculos tuos consulueris, diversum iudicabis. Vides enim multa in piis quae te offendunt, vides eos quandoque labi, peccare, infirmos esse in fide, iracundia, invidia et aliis malis affectibus laborare -: Ergo Ecclesia non est sancta. Nego consequentiam. Si meam vel proximi personam inspicio, nunquam erit sancta. Si autem Christum, Propiciatorem et Purgatorem Ecclesiae, inspicio, tota sancta est; hic enim peccata totius mundi sustulit.

Ideo peccata non sunt re vera ibi, ubi cernuntur et sentiuntur. Nam secundum Theologiam Pauli nullum peccatum, nulla mors, nulla

maledictio est amplius in mundo, sed in Christo, qui est Agnus Dei qui
tollit peccata mundi, Qui factus est maledictum, ut nos a maledicto lib-
eraret. Contra secundum Philosophiam et rationem peccatum, mors
etc. nusquam sunt nisi in mundo, in carne, in peccatoribus. Neque enim
aliter potest Sophistica Theologia considerare peccatum quam meta-
physice, nempe sic: Qualitas haeret in substantia vel subiecto; Sicut ergo
color in pariete, ita peccatum in mundo, carne vel conscientia haeret.
Igitur eluendum est per contrarios motus, scilicet per charitatem. Vera
autem Theologia docet, quod nullum peccatum amplius sit in mundo,
quia Christus in quem Pater coniecit peccata totius mundi, Esa. 53. Cap.,
vicit, delevit et occidit illud in corpore suo. Is semel mortuus peccato,
resuscitatus vero ex mortuis, amplius non moritur. Ubicunque igitur
est fides in Christum, ibi re vera peccatum abolitum, mortuum et sep-
ultum est. Ubi vero non est fides in Christum, ibi peccatum manet." WA
40/1:444, 30–445, 34.

11. *Lectures on Galatians* (1535), *LW* 26:282. WA 40/1:441, 25-27.

12. "Ista sunt capitalia nostrae theologiae, quae obscuraverunt
Sophistae. Et hic vides, quam necesse sit articulus: filium Dei Christum.
Ubi quem negavit Arius, necesse cadere ab articulo redemptionis. Nam
'vincere peccatum in seipso' *g̈ehort her zu,* quando 'homo.' Ergo oportet
sit verus deus. Lex, mors, ira ut destruerentur, *mus* divina potentia sein;
dare vitam in seipso, *das mus* divinitas; Annihilare et creare est divinae
maiestatis. Cum ergo dicat scriptura, quod destruxerit mortem, peccatum in seipso et dederit vitam. Ergo qui incipiunt negare divinitatem
Christi, postea amittunt totum Christianismum, facti Turcae. Ideo saepe
dixi, ut bene discatis articulum iustificationis. Interim donec docemus
per Christum iustificari, cogimur ostendere Christum verum dei filium.
Das sind speculationes nostrae, quae non inutiles et valent contra iustificationem operum." WA 40/1:441, 1-12 (lecture notes).

13. See, e.g., *Lectures on Galatians* (1535), *LW* 26:100. WA 40/1:182,
15.

14. *Lectures on Galatians* (1535), *LW* 26:134. "Quare Christianus
proprie definitus est liber ab omnibus legibus et nulli prorsus nec intus
nec foris subiectus. Sed significanter dico: in quantum Christianus (non
inquantum masculus aut foemina), hoc est, in quantum habet conscientiam imbutam, ornatam et ditatam illa fide, illo magno et incompre-
hensibili thesauro, vel, ut Paulus ait, 'inenarrabili dono.' Ideo non potest
illud satis magnifieri et laudari, quia facit filios et heredes Dei. Hinc

Christianus etiam maior est toto mundo, quia hoc parvum, ut videtur, donum habet in corde, sed parvitas huius doni et pretii quod in fide tenet maior est coelo et terra, quia Christus maior est qui hoc donum est." WA 40/1:235, 26–236, 16 (published text).

15. "Das ist je ein treffliche, schöne, und (wie S. Petrus sagt 2. Petri 1.) der tewren und aller groessesten Verheissungen eine, uns armen, elenden Sündern geschenkt, das wir auch Goetlicher natur teilhafftig werden sollen und so hoch geadelt, das wir nicht allein durch Christum sollen von Gott geliebet werden, sein gunst und Gnad als das hoehest, tewrest Heiligthumb haben, sondern jn, den Herrn selbs, gantz in uns wonend haben, Denn es sol (wil er sagen) nicht allein bey der Liebe bleiben, das er seinen zorn von uns nimpt und ein gnedig, Veterlich hertz gegen uns tregt, sondern wir sollen der selben Liebe auch geniessen (sonst were es uns ein vergebne, verlorne Liebe, wie das Sprichwort sagt, Lieben und nicht geniessen etc.) und grossen nutz und schatz davon haben, und sol solcher nachdruck sein, das sich solche Liebe beweise mit der that und grossem geschenk." *Crucigers Sommerpostille* (1544), WA 21:458, 11-22.

16. "Und wir so erfullet werden, 'mit allerley Gottes fulle', das ist auff Ebreische weyse soviel geredt: das wir erfullet werden auff alle weise, damit er voll macht und voll Gotes werden uberschuttet mit allen gaben und gnade und erfullet mit seynem geyst, der uns mutig mache und mit seynem liecht erleucht und seyn leben ynn uns lebe, seyne selickeit uns selig mache, seyne liebe yn uns die liebe erwecke, Kurtz umb, das alles, was er ist und vermag, ynn uns vollig sey und krefftig wircke . . ." *Predigt* (1525), WA 17/1:438, 14-28.

Chapter 2: Faith Formed by Christ

1. The following presentation is based, above all, on Luther's exposition of Gal. 2:16, which includes a comprehensive critique of scholastic theology. [Because of the modern connotations of the English word "charity," "love" is used in the following for the Latin word "caritas."— Ed.]

2. See, e.g., *Lectures on Galatians* (1535), *LW* 26:129; WA 40/1:229, 2.

3. *Lectures on Galatians* (1535), *LW* 26:129; WA 40/1:228, 12f.

4. *Lectures on Galatians* (1535), *LW* 26:129–30; WA 40/1:229, 9; 18–21.

5. *Lectures on Galatians* (1535), *LW* 26:127–28; WA 40/1:226, 14-19.

6. *Lectures on Galatians* (1535), *LW* 26:130; WA 40/1:229, 9.

7. This expression is used, for example, in the following: Heiko Obermann. "'Iustitia Christi' und 'Iustitia Dei': Luther und die scholastischen Lehren von der Rechtfertigung," *Der Durchbruch der reformatorischen Erkenntnis bei Luther,* ed. Bernhard Lohse (Darmstadt: Wissenschaftliche Buchgesellschaft, 1968) 423.

8. *Lectures on Galatians* (1535), *LW* 26:129–30 (translation modified). "Nos autem loco charitatis istius ponimus fidem, Et sicut ipsi dicunt fidem MONOGRAMMA et charitatem vivos colores et plenitudinem ipsam, ita nos e contra dicimus fidem apprehendere Christum qui est forma, quae fidem ornat et informat, ut color parietem. Quare fides Christiana non est otiosa qualitas vel vacua siliqua in corde quae possit existere in peccato mortali, donec charitas accedat et eam vivificet, Sed si est vera fides, est quaedam certa fiducia cordis et firmus assensus quo Christus apprehenditur, Sic ut Christus sit obiectum fidei, imo non obiectum, sed, ut ita dicam, in ipsa fide Christus adest. Fides ergo est cognitio quaedam vel tenebra quae nihil videt, Et tamen in istis tenebris Christus fide apprehensus sedet, Quemadmodum Deus in Sinai et in Templo sedebat in medio tenebrarum. Est ergo formalis nostra iustitia non charitas informans fidem, sed ipsa fides et nebula cordis, hoc est, fiducia in rem quam non videmus, hoc est, in Christum qui, ut maxime non videatur, tamen praesens est.

Iustificat ergo fides, quia apprehendit et possidet istum thesaurum, scilicet Christum praesentem. Sed quo modo praesens sit, non est cogitabile, quia sunt tenebrae, ut dixi. Ubi ergo vera fiducia cordis est, ibi adest Christus in ipsa nebula et fide. Eaque est formalis iustitia propter quam homo iustificatur, non propter charitatem, ut Sophistae loquuntur. Summa: Sicut Sophistae dicunt charitatem formare et imbuere fidem, Sic nos dicimus Christum formare et imbuere fidem vel formam esse fidei. Ergo fide apprehensus et in corde habitans Christus est iustitia Christiana propter quam Deus nos reputat iustos et donat vitam aeternam. Ibi certe nullum est opus legis, nulla dilectio, sed longe alia iustitia et novus quidam mundus extra et supra legem; Christus enim vel fides non est Lex nec opus legis." WA 40/1:228, 27–229, 32.

9. On the concept of "absolute" faith see the following study: Regin Prenter, "Luthers Lehre von der Heiligung," *Lutherforschung heute,* ed. Vilmos Vajta (Berlin: Lutherisches Verlagshaus, 1958) 66.

10. *Prefaces to the New Testament, LW* 35:370. "Aber Glaub ist eyn gotlich werck ynn uns, das uns wandelt und neu gepirt aus Gott, Johan.1.

und todtet den allten Adam, macht uns gantz ander menschen von hertz, mut synn und allen krefften, und bringet den heyligen geyst mit sich. O es ist eyn lebendig, schefftig, thettig, mechtig ding umb den glauben, das unmuglich ist, das er nicht on unterlass solt gutts wircken." WA,DB 7:10, 6-10.

11. *Lectures on Galatians* (1535), *LW* 26:357 (translation modified). "Ea est vera fides Christi et in Christum, per quam membra fimus corporis eius, de carne et ossibus eius. Ergo in ipso vivimus, movemur et sumus. Ideo vana est Sectariorum speculatio de fide qui somniant Christum spiritualiter, hoc est, speculative in nobis esse, realiter vero in coelis. Oportet Christum et fidem omnino coniungi, oportet simpliciter nos in coelo versari et Christum esse, vivere et operari in nobis; vivit autem et operatur in nobis non speculative, sed realiter, praesentissime et efficacissime." WA 40/1:546, 21-28.

12. *Lectures on Galatians* (1535), *LW* 26:356. "Phanatici spiritus hodie loquuntur more Sophistarum de fide in Christum somniantes eam esse qualitatem haerentem in corde, excluso Christo. Is perniciosus error est. Verum ita proponendus est Christus, ut praeter eum plane nihil videas, nihil tibi esse proprius et intimius ipso credas. Non enim sedet ociosus in coelis, sed praesentissimus est nobis, operans et vivens in nobis, Supra Cap. 2: 'Vivo iam non ego, sed vivit in me Christus' etc., Et hic: 'Christum induistis.'" WA 40/1:545, 24-30.

Chapter 3: The Law and Participation in the "Divine Life"

1. *Lectures on Galatians* (1535), *LW* 26:403–4. "Et qui vellet hic Rhetoricari, posset haec verba latissime amplificare Active, Passive et Neutraliter. Active: lex est elementum infirmum et egenum, quia reddit homines infirmiores et egentiores. Passive: quia ipsa per se non habet vim et opes iustitiae donandae vel afferendae. Et per se neutraliter est infirmitas et paupertas, quae homines infirmos et pauperes semper magis magisque affligit et excrutiat. Ideo per legem velle iustificari idem est, ac si quis alioqui infirmus et aeger accerseret sibi praeterea grandius aliquod malum, quod eum prorsus enecaret, et tamen interim diceret se per hoc velle medicari aegritudinem suam, Ut si laborans morbo comitiali adiungat sibi pestem, Aut si leprosus ad leprosum, mendicus ad mendicum veniret, alter opem laturus alteri et locupletaturus illum. Horum alter, iuxta proverbium, mulgeret hircum, alter supponeret cribrum." WA 40/1:613, 23–614, 16 (published text).

2. *Lectures on Galatians* (1535), *LW* 26:406–7. "Quod velle iustificari ex lege sit Ex vacuo loculo pecuniam numerare, Ex vacuo vase et cantharo edere et bibere, Ibi robur et opes quaerere, ubi mera est infirmitas et paupertas, Aggravare oppressum et succumbentem oneri, Centum aureos velle solvere et ne nummum quidem habere, Nudo vestem exuere, Aegrum et egentem maiore infirmitate et inopia opprimere etc." WA 40/1:617, 25-30.

3. *Lectures on Galatians* (1535), *LW* 26:404. "Ideo omnis homo deficiens a promissione ad legem, a fide ad opera nihil aliud facit, quam quod sibi infirmo et egenti imponat iugum importabile, Act. 15., quo gestando decuplo fit infirmior et egentior, donec tandem desperet, nisi Christus veniat et liberet eum.

Hoc idem testatur Evangelium de Muliere, quae duodecim annos laboraverat profluvio sanguinis et multa perpessa fuerat a compluribus medicis, in quos insumpserat omnem substantiam suam, nec tamen poterat ab illis curari, sed quo longius curabatur, hoc peius habebat etc. Quotquot igitur hoc nomine faciunt opera Legis, ut per ea iustificentur, illi non solum non iusti, sed dulpiciter iniusti redduntur, Hoc est, ut dixi, infirmiores, egentiores et ineptiores ad omne opus bonum redduntur per legem etc. Hoc ipse expertus sum in me et multis aliis. Nam in Papatu plerosque ex Monachis vidi, qui ardentissimo studio multa et grandia opera faciebant pro acquirenda iustitia et salute, et tamen nihil erat illis impatientius, infirmius, miserius, nihil magis incredulum, pavidum et desperabundum. Magistratus politici, qui versabantur in maximis et gravissimis causis, non erant tam impatientes et tam muliebriter impotentes, non erant tam superstitiosi, increduli, pavidi etc., ut eiusmodi iustitiarii." WA 40/1:614, 28–615, 19 (published text).

4. *Lectures on Galatians* (1535), *LW* 27:13–14. "... recedunt a iusticia et vita longius quam Publicani, Peccatores et Meretrices. Illi enim non possunt niti fiducia operum suorum, cum talia sint, propter quae non possint confidere se consecuturos gratiam et remissionem peccatorum: Nam si iustitia et opera secundum legem facta non iustificant, multo minus peccata contra legem commissa iustificant. Sunt igitur feliciores hac in parte iusticiariis, quia deest eis propriorum operum fiducia, quae si non penitus tollit fidem in Christum, tamen maxime eam impedit. E contra Iusticiarii abstinentes externe a peccatis et in speciem inculpate et religiose viventes non possunt carere opinione fiduciae et iusticiae, cum qua stare non potest fides in Christum. Ideoque infeliciores sunt

publicanis et meretricibus, qui Deo irato non offerunt sua bona opera, ut pro eis reddat ipsis vitam aeternam (ut Operarii), cum nulla habeant, sed ignosci sibi sua peccata propter Christum petunt etc." WA 40/2:15, 28–16, 18 (published text).

5. *Lectures on Galatians* (1535), *LW* 26:366. "Discat igitur pius Legem et Christum duo contraria esse, prorsus incompatibilia: praesente Christo lex nullo modo dominari, sed cedere debet e conscientia et relinquere cubile (quod angustius est, quam ut duos possit capere, Esai. 28.) soli Christo. Is solus dominetur in iustitia, securitate, laetitia et vita, ut conscientia laeta obdormiat in Christo sine ullo sensu legis, peccati et mortis." WA 40/1:558, 33–559, 15 (published text).

6. *Lectures on Galatians* (1535), *LW* 26:314. ". . . (Lex) Deinde aperit homini cognitionem sui. . . . Sic ergo lex ministra et praeparatrix est ad gratiam. Nam Deus est Deus humilium, miserorum, afflictorum, oppressorum, desperatorum et eorum qui prorsus in nihilum redacti sunt; Estque Dei natura exaltare humiles, cibare esurientes, illuminare caecos, miseros et afflictos consolari, peccatores iustificare, mortuos vivificare, desperatos et damnatos salvare etc. Est enim Creator omnipotens ex nihilo faciens omnia." WA 40/1:487, 32–488, 19 (published text).

7. *Lectures on Galatians* (1535), *LW* 26:364. "Quare Lex Mosi nihil praeter mundana praestat hoc est, ostendit Civiliter et Theologice tantum mala quae in mundo sunt. Urget tamen, suis terroribus conscientiam, ut sitiat et quaerat promissionem Dei et intueatur in Christum. Sed ad eam rem requiritur Spiritus sanctus, qui dicat in corde: Non est voluntas Dei, postquam lex fecit officium suum in te, ut tantum terrearis et occidaris, sed ut per legem agnoscens miseriam et perditionem tuam, non tamen desperes, sed credas in Christum qui est finis legis ad iustitiam omni credenti. Hic plane nihil mundani donatur, sed cessant hic omnia mundana, omnes leges, et incipiunt divina." WA 40/1:556, 20-28.

8. *Lectures on Galatians* (1535), *LW* 26:163 (emphasis added). "Sic Christus suavissimis appellationibus vocatur mea Lex, Peccatum meum, Mors mea, contra legem, peccatum, mortem, cum revera nihil sit quam mera libertas, iustitia, vita et salus aeterna. Ideo autem factus est Lex legi, peccatum peccato, mors morti, ut me a maledicto legis redimeret, iustificaret et vivificaret me. Sic utroque modo Christus dum est Lex, est libertas, dum est peccatum, est iustitia, dum est mors, est vita. hoc ipso enim, quod passus est se legem accusare, peccatum damnare, mortem devorare, legem abrogavit, peccatum damnavit, mortem destruxit, me

iustificavit et salvavit. Sic Christus simul est venenum contra legem, peccatum et mortem et remedium pro libertate, iustitia et vita aeterna." WA 40/1:556, 20-28.

Chapter 4: Christ and the Believer as One Person

1. *Lectures on Galatians* (1535), *LW* 26:167. "Non ego iam in mea persona vivo, sed 'Christus in me vivit'. Persona quidem vivit, sed non in se aut pro sua persona. Sed quis est ille Ego, de quo dicit: 'Iam non Ego'? Is Ego est qui legem habet et operari debet quique est persona quaedam segregata a Christo. Illum Ego Paulus reiicit, Quia Ego ut distincta persona a Christo pertinet ad mortem et Infernum. Ideo inquit: 'Iam non Ego, sed Christus in me vivit'; Is est mea forma ornans fidem meam, ut color vel lux parietem ornat. (Sic crasse illa exponenda est; Non enim possumus spiritualiter comprehendere tam proxime et intime Christum haerere et manere in nobis, quam lux vel albedo in pariete haeret.) Christus ergo, inquit, sic inhaerens et conglutinatus mihi et manens in me hanc vitam quam ago, vivit in me, imo vita qua sic vivo, est Christus ipse. Itaque Christus et ego iam unum in hac parte sumus." WA 40/1:283, 20-32 (published text).

2. *Lectures on Galatians* (1535), *LW* 26:167. "Vivens autem in me Christus abolet legem, peccatum damnat, mortem mortificat, quia ad praesentiam ipsius illa non possunt non evanescere. Est enim Christus aeterna pax, consolatio, iustitia et vita; His autem cedere oportet terrorem legis, moerorem animi, peccatum, Infernum, mortem. Sic Christus in me manens et vivens tollit et absorbet omnia mala quae me cruciant et affligunt. Quare haec inhaerentia facit, ut liberer a terroribus legis et peccati, eximar e cute mea et transferar in Christum ac in illius regnum, quod est regnum gratiae, iustitiae, pacis, gaudii, vitae, salutis et gloriae aeternae; in illo autem agens, nihil mali potest nocere mihi." WA 40/1:283, 33–284, 19 (published text).

3. *Lectures on Galatians* (1535), *LW* 26:167–68. "Interim foris quidem manet vetus homo, subiectus legi; sed quantum attinet ad iustificationem, oportet Christum et me esse coniunctissimos, ut ipse in me vivat et ego in illo (Mirabilis est haec loquendi ratio). Quia vero in me vivit, ideo, quidquid in me est gratiae, iustitiae, vitae, pacis, salutis, est ipsius Christi, et tamen illud ipsum meum est per conglutationem et inhaesionem quae est per fidem, per quam efficimur quasi unum corpus in spiritu. Quia ergo vivit in me Christus, necesse est simul cum eo adesse

gratiam, iustitiam, vitam ac salutem aeternam et abesse legem, peccatum, mortem, Imo legem a lege, peccatum a peccato, mortem a morte, Diabolum a Diabolo crucifigi, devorari et aboleri. Sic Paulus conatur nos prorsus abstrahere a nobisipsis, a lege et operibus et in ipsum Christum et fidem Christi transplantare, ut nihil plane spectemus in ratione iustificande quam gratiam et eam longissime separemus a lege et operibus, quae procul hic abesse debent." WA 40/1:284, 20-33.

4. [and is an image used by mystics—Ed.]

5. *Lectures on Galatians* (1535), *LW* 26:168–69. "Verum recte docenda est fides, quod per eam sic conglutineris Christo, ut ex te et ipso fiat quasi una persona quae non possit segregari sed perpetuo adhaerescat ei et dicat: Ego sum ut Christus, et vicissim Christus dicat: Ego sum ille peccator, quia adhaeret mihi, et ego illi; Coniuncti enim sumus per fidem in unam carnem et os, Eph. 5.: 'Membra sumus corporis Christi, de carne eius et de ossibus eius.' Ita, ut haec fides Christum et me arctius copulet, quam maritus est uxori copulatus. Ergo fides illa non est otiosa qualitas, sed tanta est eius magnitudo, ut obscuret et prorsus tollat ista stultissima somnia doctrinae Sophisticae de fictione fidei formatae et charitatis, de meritis, de dignitate aut qualitate nostra etc." WA 40/1:285, 24–286, 20 (published text).

The postscript is even stronger: "Sed fides facit ex te et Christo quasi unam personam, ut non segregeris a Christo, imo in horescas, quasi dicaste Christum, et contra: ego sum ille peccator, quia inheret mihi et contra." WA 40/1:285, 5-7.

6. *Lectures on Galatians* (1535), *LW* 26:168 (emphasis added). "Est enim plane insolens et inaudita, Ut: 'Vivo', 'non vivo'; 'mortuus sum', 'non mortuus sum'; sum peccator, non sum peccator; habeo legem, non habeo legem. Sed ista phrasis vera est in Christo et per Christum. Quare si in causa iustificationis discernis personam Christi et tuam, tum es in lege, manes in ea et vivis in te, quod est mortuum esse apud Deum et damnari a lege, . . ." WA 40/1:285, 12-17.

Chapter 5: "Through Faith One Becomes God"

1. *Lectures on Galatians* (1535), *LW* 26:100; WA 40/1:182, 15.

2. *Lectures on Galatians* (1535), *LW* 26:247, 248. "Fidelis plane est divinus homo, filius Dei, heres orbis terrarum; Est victor mundi, peccati, mortis, diaboli etc., ideo satis laudari non potest." "Credens igitur Abraham implet coelum et terram. Sic unusquisque Christianus implet coelum et terram fide sua." WA 40/1:390, 22-24.

3. *Lectures on Galatians* (1535), *LW* 26:134; WA 40/1:235, 15–236, 16.

4. *The Freedom of a Christian* (1520), *LW* 31:354. "Wie nu Christus die erste gepurtt hatt/ mit yhrer ehre vnd wirdickeit/ alßo/ teyllet er sie mit allenn seynen Christen/ das sie durch den glauben/ mussen auch alle kuenige vnd priester seyn/ mit Christo/ Wie Sankt Petrus sagt 1. Pet. 2. Ihr seyt ein priesterlich kuenigreych/ und ein kueniglich priesterthum, Vnd das geht also zu/ das ein Christen mensch durch den glauben ßo hoch erhaben wirt vbir alle ding/ das er aller eyn herr wirt geystlich/ denn es kann yhm kein ding nit schaden zur seligkeit. Ja es muß yhm alles vnterthan seyn vnd helffen zur seligkeit/ Wie Sankt Paulus leret Ro. 8. Alle ding muessen helffenn den außerwelten/ zu yhrem besten/ es sey leben sterben/ sund/ frumkeit gut vnd boeßes/ wie man es nennen kan. Item 1. Cor.3. Alle ding seynd ewr/ es sey leben oder der todt/ kegenwertig oder zukuenfftig etcetera." *Von der Freiheit eines Christenmenschen.* Studienausgabe 2, 281, 1-12. WA 7:27, 17-28. [The translation in *LW* is based on the Latin version of the text in the WA.—Ed.]

5. *Lectures on Galatians* (1535), *LW* 27:74. "Christianus fit artifex potentissimus et mirificus Creator, qui ex tristicia gaudium, ex terroribus consolationem, ex peccato insticiam, ex morte vitam . . . facere potest." WA 40/2:93, 29-31.

6. *In epistolam S. Pauli ad Galatas Commentarius ex praelectione D. Martini Luther collectus* (1535), WA 40/1:650, 3; 651, 3.

7. "Und wir so erfullet werden, 'mit allerley Gottes fulle', das ist auff Ebreische weyse soviel geredt: das wir erfullet werden auff alle weise, damit er voll macht und voll Gotes werden uberschuttet mit allen gaben und gnade und erfullet mit seynem geyst, der uns mutig mache und mit seynem liecht erleucht und seyn leben ynn uns lebe, seyne selickeit uns selig mache, seyne liebe yn uns die liebe erwecke, Kurtz umb, das alles, was er ist und vermag, ynn uns vollig sey und krefftig wircke, das wir gantz vergottet werden, nicht eyn partecken odder allein etliche stuck Gottes habt, sondern alle fulle. Es ist viel davon geschrieben, wie der mensch soll vergottet werden, da haben sie leytern gemacht, daran man gen hymel steyge und viel solchs dings, Es ist aber eytel pertecken werck, hie ist aber der rechte und nehiste weg hynan zu komen angezeygt, das du voll Gottes werdest, das dirs as keynem stuck feyle, sondern alles auff eynen hauffen habist, das alles, was du redist, denckist, gehist, summa: deyn gantzes leben gar Gottisch sey." *Predigt* (1525), WA 17/1:438, 14-28 (emphasis added).

8. *Lectures on Galatians* (1535), *LW* 26:266. "Sit ergo in Theologia fides perpetuo divinitas operum et sic perfusa per opera, ut divinitas per humanitatem in Christo. Qui in ferro ignito attingit ignem, ferrum attingit. Ita qui tetigit cutem Christi, vere Deum tetigit. Est ergo fides Factotum (ut ita loquar) in operibus." WA 40/1:417, 15-19.

9. *Galaterkommentar* (1535), WA 40/1:417, 13; *LW* 26:266: "concrete, composite, and incarnate faith."

10. *In epistolam S. Pauli ad Galatas Commentarius ex praelectione D. Martini Luther collectus* (1535), WA 40/1:20, 29.

Chapter 6: The Presence of Christ and Sanctification

1. *Lectures on Galatians* (1535), *LW* 26:170. "Est igitur duplex vita: Mea naturalis vel animalis, et aliena, scilicet Christi in me. Secundum animalem meam vitam mortuus sum, iamque vivo alienam vitam. Non vivo iam Paulus, sed Paulus mortuus est. Quis tum vivit? Christianus. Paulus ergo ut in se vivens plane per legem mortuus est, Sed ut in Christo vel potius ut Christus in eo vivens vivit aliena vita, quia Christus in eo loquitur, operatur et exercet omnes actiones." WA 40/1:287, 28-33.

2. *Lectures on Galatians* (1535), *LW* 26:171. "Ergo quantulacunque est, inquit, ista vita quam in carne vivo, in fide filii Dei vivo, Id est, hoc verbum quod corporaliter sono, est verbum non carnis sed Spiritus sancti et Christi. Iste visus qui ingreditur vel egreditur ex oculis, non venit ex carne, hoc est, caro mea non regit eum sed spiritus sanctus. Ita auditus non ex carne, licet in carne sit, sed in et ex spiritu sancto est. Christianus non loquitur nisi casta, sobria, sancta ac divina, quae pertinent ad Christum, ad gloriam Dei et ad salutem proximi. Ista non veniunt ex carne neque fiunt secundum carnem, et tamen sunt in carne. Non enim possum docere, praedicare, scribere, orare, gratias agere nisi istis instrumentis carnis quae requiruntur ad talia opera perficienda; Et tamen ea non veniunt ex carne neque in ea nascuntur, sed donantur et revelantur e coelo divinitus. Sic aspicio oculis mulierculam, sed casto visu, non cupiens eam. Illa visio non venit ex carne, quanquam sit in carne, quia oculi sunt instrumentum carnale illius visionis, sed castitas illa visionis e coelo venit." WA 40/1:289, 16-30.

3. *Lectures on Galatians* (1535), *LW* 26:172. "Ex his intelligi quod est, unde veniat illa aliena et spiritualis vita quam animalis homo non percipit. Nescit enim, qualis haec sit vita; Ventum quidem audit sonantem, sed unde veniat aut quo vadat, nescit. Audit vocem spiritualis hominis,

agnoscit faciem, mores et gestus eius, Sed unde illa verba non sacrilega et blasphema ut antea, sed sancta et divina, Unde illi motus et actiones veniant, non videt, Quia illa vita est in corde per fidem, ubi exstincta carne regnat Christus cum suo spiritu sancto, qui iam videt, audit, loquitur, operatur, patitur et simpliciter omnia agit in ipso, etiamsi caro reluctetur. Breviter, ista vita non est carnis, licet sit in carne, sed Christi filii Dei, quem fide possidet Christianus." WA 40/1:290, 22-31.

4. *In epistolam S. Pauli ad Galatas Commentarius ex praelectione D. Martini Luther collectus* (1535), WA 40/1:23, 9-23.

5. *Lectures on Galatians* (1535), *LW* 26:255. "Quare is verus est factor Legis qui accepto Spiritu sancto per fidem Christi incipit diligere Deum et benefacere proximo, Ut facere includat simul fidem, quae fides habet ipsum facientem et facit arborem, qua facta fiunt fructus. Oportet enim prius esse arborem, deinde fructus. Poma enim non faciunt arborem, sed arbor poma facit. Sic fides primum personam facit quae postea facit opera. Itaque facere Legem absque fide est facere poma sine arbore ex ligno et luto, quod non est facere poma sed mera phantasmata. Posita autem arbore, hoc est persona seu factore qui fit per fidem in Christum, sequuntur opera." WA 40/1:401, 30–402, 20.

6. *Lectures on Galatians* (1535), *LW* 26:266–67 (emphasis added). "Theologicum opus est fidele opus. Sic homo Theologicus est fidelis, item ratio recta, voluntas bona est fidelis ratio et voluntas, Ut fides in universum sit divinitas in opere, persona et membris, ut unica causa iustificationis quae postea etiam tribuitur materiae propter formam, hoc est, operi propter fidem. Ut regnum divinitatis traditur Christo homini non propter humanitatem, sed divinitatem. Sola enim divinitas creavit omnia humanitate nihil cooperante; Sicut neque peccatum et mortem humanitas vicit, sed hamus qui latebat sub vermiculo, in quem diabolus impegit, vicit et devoravit diabolum qui erat devoraturus vermiculum. Itaque sola humanitas nihil effecisset, sed divinitas humanitati coniuncta sola fecit et humanitas propter divinitatem. Sic hic sola fides iustificat et facit omnia; Et tamen operibus idem tribuitur propter fidem." WA 40/1:417, 25–418, 11 (published text).

7. *Lectures on Galatians* (1535), *LW* 26:272–73. "Quare fides perpetuo iustificat et vivificat, et tamen non manet sola, id est, otiosa. Non quod non sola in suo gradu et officio maneat, quia perpetuo sola iustificat, sed incarnatur et fit homo, hoc est, non est et manet otiosa vel sine charitate. Sic Christus secundum divinitatem et substantia vel natura divina

et aeterna sine principio, Humanitas vero est natura in tempore creata. Hae duae naturae in Christo sunt inconfusae et impermixtae et utriusque proprium est distincte intelligendum. Humanitatis est incepisse in tempore, Divinitatis est esse aeternum sine principio; Et tamen conveniunt haec duo et incorporatur divinitas sine principio in humanitatem cum principio. Ut ergo distinguere cogor inter humanitatem et divinitatem et dicere: Humanitas non est divinitas, Et tamen homo est Deus, Ita hic distinguo: lex non est fides et tamen fides operatur et conveniunt fides et opera in concreto vel composito et tamen utrumque habet et servat suam naturam et proprium officium." WA 40/1:427, 11-24.

8. *Lectures on Galatians* (1535), *LW* 26:401; WA 40/1:610, 15-18.

9. *Lectures on Galatians* (1535), *LW* 26:260. "Sumus ille vulneratus qui incidit in latrones, cuius vulnera Samaritanus obligavit infundes oleum et vinum, quem deinde imponens in iumentum suum duxit in diversorium curamque illius egit, Abiens autem commendavit eum hospiti dicens: 'curam illius habe.' Itaque fovemur interim tanquam in hospitali, donec adiiciat Dominus secundo manum, ut Esaias ait, ut liberet nos." WA 40/1:408, 16-21.

Chapter 7: "Simultaneously Righteous and a Sinner"

1. [We are here considering the issue of declared and real righteousness as it applies to a Christian who already believes. The issue of how faith begins, and in whom, is not discussed here.—Ed.]

2. *Lectures on Galatians* (1535), *LW* 26:229; WA 40/1:364, 11.

3. *In epistolam S. Pauli ad Galatas Commentarius ex praelectione D. Martini Luther collectus* (1535). WA 40 I; 363, 9. "Faith is indeed a formal righteousness." *Lectures on Galatians* (1535), LW 26, 229.

4. *Lectures on Galatians* (1535), *LW* 26:132–33 (translation modified). "Et valde necessaria est Acceptatio seu reputatio, Primum, quia nondum sumus pure iusti, sed in hac vita haeret adhuc peccatum in carne. Hoc reliquum in carne peccatum purgat in nobis Deus. Deinde relinquimur quandoque etiam a Spiritu sancto et labimur in peccata ut Petrus, Davis et alii Sancti. Habemus tamen semper regressum ad istum articulum, quod peccata nostra tecta sint quodque Deus ea non velit nobis imputare, Ro. 4. Non quod peccatum non adsit (ut Sophistae docuerunt Tamdiu bene operandum esse, donec nobis conscii simus nullius peccati), sed peccatum adest vere et pii illud sentiunt, sed ignoratur et absconditum est apud Deum obstante Mediatore Christo, quem quia fide

apprehendimus, oportet omnia peccata non esse peccata." WA 40/1:233, 25–234, 15.

5. *In epistolam S. Pauli ad Galatas Commentarius ex praelectione D. Martini Luther collectus* (1535), WA 40/1:364, 8-9. "Faith begins righteousness, but imputation perfects it until the day of Christ." *Lectures on Galatians* (1535), *LW* 26:230.

6. "Mach differentiam nu: quae fides ei reputatur ad iusticiam propter Christum. 1. fides est donum divinitus datum, qua credo in Christum. 2. pars: quod deus reputat istam imperfectam fidem ad iustitiam perfectam. Ipse proponit in oculum suum filium suum passum, in quem cepi credere. Interim dum vivo in carne, est peccatum in me, sed propter fidem in Christum non videtur, est ibi laquear, quae dicitur remissio peccatorum, quod deus non potest videre. Sum peccator, caro mea irascitur, non laetatur in deo, irascitur; sed nescit de eis peccatis, sed sum apud eum, quasi non essent peccata. Hoc facit reputatio." *In epistolam S. Pauli ad Galatas Commentarius ex praelectione D. Martini Luther collectus* (1535), WA 40/1:366, 7–367, 6 (lecture notes).

7. *Lectures on Galatians* (1535), *LW* 26:234; WA 40/1:3–4 (emphasis added).

8. *Lectures on Galatians* (1535), *LW* 26:130 (emphasis added; translation modified). "Iustificat ergo fides, quia apprehendit et possidet istum thesaurum, scilicet Christum praesentem. Sed quo modo praesens sit, non est cogitabile, quia sunt tenebrae, ut dixi. Ubi ergo vera fiducia cordis est, ibi adest Christus in ipsa nebula et fide. Eaque est formalis iustitia propter quam homo iustificatur, non propter charitatem, ut Sophistae loquuntur. Summa: Sicut Sophistae dicunt charitatem formare et imbuere fidem, Sic nos dicimus Christum formare et imbuere fidem vel formam esse fidei. Ergo fide apprehensus et in corde habitans Christus est iustitia Christiana propter quam Deus nos reputat iustos et donat vitam aeternam. Ibi certe nullum est opus legis, nulla dilectio, sed longe alia iustitia et novus quidam mundus extra et supra legem; Christus enim vel fides non est Lex nec opus legis." WA 40/1:229, 22-32.

9. [*LW*: "by means of"—Ed.]

10. *Lectures on Galatians* (1535), *LW* 26:132 (translation modified). "Est et hic notandum, quod ista tria, Fides, Christus, Acceptio vel Reputatio, coiuncta sunt. Fides enim apprehendit Christum et habet eum praesentem includitque eum ut annulus gemmam, Et qui fuerit inventus cum tali fide apprehensi Christi in corde, illum reputat Deus iustum. Haec

ratio est et meritum, quo pervenimus ad remissionem peccatorum et iustitiam. Quia credis, inquit Deus, in me et fides tua apprehendit Christum quem tibi donavi, ut esset Iustificator et Salvator tuus, ideo sis iustus. Itaque Deus acceptat seu reputat te iustum, solum propter Christum in quem credis etc." WA 40/1:233, 16-24.

11. *Lectures on Galatians* (1535), *LW* 26:350 (translation modified). "Accepimus igitur primitias Spiritus et fermentum absconditum est in massam, sed tota massa nondum fermentata est, sed coepit fermentari. Si inspicio fermentum, nihil video nisi merum fermentum, si corpus massae, nondum est merum fermentum. Sic, si Christum inspicio, totus sanctus et purus sum, nihil plane sciens de lege, Christus enim est fermentum meum. Si vero meam carnem inspicio, sentio avaritiam, libidinem, iram, superbiam etc., Timorem mortis, tristitiam, pavorem, odium, murmurationem et impatientiam contra Deum. Quatenus ista adsunt, eatenus abest Christus, aut si adest, infirme adest. Hic opus est adhuc paedagogo qui fortem asinum, Carnem, exerceat et vexet, ut hac paedagogia minuantur peccata et Christo via paretur. Christus enim, ut semel secundum tempus corporaliter venit, totam legem abrogavit, peccatum abolevit, mortem et infernum destruxit, Ita spiritualiter sine intermissione ad nos venit et ista perpetuo in nobis exstinguit atque occidit." WA 40/1:537, 21-34.

12. *Lectures on Galatians* (1535), *LW* 26:350–51. "Verum est, quatenus Christum inspicis, re vera lex et peccatum abolita sunt. Sed Christus nondum venit tibi, aut si venit, tamen adhuc reliquiae peccati in te sunt, nondum fermentatus es totus. Ubi enim est concupiscentia, tristitia spiritus, pavor mortis etc., ibi adhuc lex et peccatum est. Christus nondum vere adest qui veniens expellit timorem et tristitiam et adfert pacem et securitatem conscientiae. Quatenus igitur Christum fide apprehendo, eatenus abrogata est mihi lex. Sed caro mea, mundus et diabolus non permittunt fidem esse perfectam. Velim quidem, quod parvula lux fidei in corde diffusa esset per totum corpus et omnia membra. Non fit, non statim diffunditur, sed coepta est diffundi. Interim ea est consolatio nostra, quod primitias Spiritus habentes incepimus fermentari, fermentabimur autem toti, cum corpus hoc peccati dissolvetur et novi cum Christo resurgemus. Amen." WA 40/1:538, 14-25. See also, e.g., WA 40/2:93, 20; WA 40/2:85, 26–86, 19; WA 40/1:93, 1.

13. *Lectures on Galatians* (1535), *LW* 26:234. "Itaque apprehendere illum filium et corde in illum credere, quod donum Dei est, facit, quod

Deus reputet illam fidem licet imperfectam pro iustitia perfecta. Et hic in alio prorsus mundo extra rationem sumus, ubi non disputatur, quid nos facere debeamus, quo genere operum gratiam et remissionem peccatorum mereamur, sed hic sumus in divina Theologia, ubi audimus hoc Evangelium, quod Christus pro nobis mortuus sit quodque hoc credentes reputemur iusti, manentibus nihilominus in nobis peccatis et quidem grandibus." WA 40/1:371, 18-25.

14. "Nu aber sind wyr da hyndurch und haben eyn hoher erkentnis des herren Christi, wer den erkennet als den man der da hilfft, der da krafft gibt das gesetz zu erfullen, durch welchen wyr haben erlanget vergebung der sunde, so spiegelt sich seyn klarheyt ynn uns, das ist: Wie der sonnen glantz sich spiegelt ynn eynem wasser odder ynn einem spiegel, also spiegelt sich Christus und gibt eynen glantz von sich yns hertz, Also das wir verklert werden von eyner klarheyt zu der andern, das wir teglich zunehmen und yhe klerer und klerer den herren erkennen, denn werden wyr verwandelt und verklert ynn das selbig byld, also das wyr alle eyn kuche werden mit christo. Das gehet nicht also zu, das wyrs selbs thun aus eygen krefften, sondern Gott mus es thun, der da der geyst ist. Denn ob schon der heylig geyst solche klarheyt und erleuchtnis ynn uns ansehet und uns darnach verlies, so weren wir wie vor." *Predigt* (1522), WA 10/3:425, 13-25.

Chapter 8: The Christian Struggle

1. *Lectures on Galatians* (1535), *LW* 27:65–67; WA 40/2:81, 26–82, 22; WA 40/2:82, 27–83, 22.

2. *Lectures on Galatians* (1535), *LW* 27:56; WA 40/2:70, 24–71, 21.

3. *Lectures on Galatians* (1535), *LW* 27:53; WA 40/2:66, 28-30. In other contexts also Luther underscores that faith brings with it not only love of neighbors but also love of God.

4. *Lectures on Galatians* (1535), *LW* 27:57–58 (translation modified). "Breve verbum est et pulchre ac potenter dictum: 'Diliges proximum tuum sicut Teipsum.' Nemo potest dare melius, certius et propius exemplum quam Seipsum. Neque dari potest nobilior et profundior habitus quam charitas, Neque excellentius obiectum quam Proximus. Exemplum ergo, habitus et obiectum sunt nobilissima. Itaque si cupis scire, quo modo diligendus sit proximus, et habere exemplum illustre huius rei, considera diligenter, quo modo Tu teipsum diligas. Certe cuperes anxie in necessitate aut periculo te amari et iuvari omnibus consiliis, facultatibus

et viribus non solum omnium hominum sed etiam omnium creaturam. Quare nullo libro indiges, qui te erudiat et admoneat, quomodo proximum diligere debeas, habes enim pulcherrimum et optimum librum omnium legum in corde tuo. Non eges ullo doctore hac in re, tantum consule tuum proprium cor, hoc satis abunde docebit te, ita diligendum esse tuum proximum, ut Teipsum. Deinde charitas summa virtus est, quae non solum parata est servire lingua, manu, pecunia, facultatibus, sed etiam corpore et ipsa vita." WA 40/2:72, 14-28.

5. *Lectures on Galatians* (1535), *LW* 27:32. "Continent autem illa verba: 'Currebatis bene' consolationem. Paulus enim respicit illis verbis ad tentationem, qua boni exercentur, quibus vita sua videtur pigra et magis reptatio quaedam quam cursus. Sed praesente sana doctrina, (quae sine fructu tractari non potest, affert enim Spiritum sanctum cum suis donis) vita piorum, etiamsi videatur reputatio, cursus quidam strenuus est. Apparet quidem nobis, omnia difficulter et tarde progredi, sed quod nobis tardum videtur, coram Deo velox est, quod nobis vix reputat, hoc illi velociter currit. Item quod in oculis nostris tristicia, peccatum, mors est, hoc apud Deum est gaudium, iusticia et vita propter Christum, per quem consummati sumus. Christus autem Sanctus, iustus, laetus etc. est nihilque ei deest, sic credentibus in eum nihil deest. Itaque Christiani vere sunt cursores et quicquid faciunt, currit et feliciter progreditur, provehente hoc Christi spiritu, qui nescit tarda molimina." WA 40/2:40, 7-19.

6. See especially Manfred Schloenbach, *Heiligung als Fortschreiten und Wachstum des Glaubens in Luthers Theologie* (Helsinki, 1963).

7. *Lectures on Galatians* (1535), *LW* 27:64. "Hoc umbraculo, coelo remissionis peccatorum et throno gratiae, conclusi et protecti incipimus diligere et implere legem. Sed propter hanc impletionem non iustificamur neque accepti sumus, dum hic vivimus. 'Ubi vero tradiderit Christus regnum Deo Patri aboleverit omnem principatum etc. et Deus erit omnia in omnibus', ibi tum cessabit fides et spes, et charitas erit perfecta et aeterna, 1. Cor. 13." WA 40/2:80, 21-26.

8. *Lectures on Galatians* (1535), *LW* 27:72–73 (translation modified). "Ideo nemo miretur aut perterrefiat, cum sentit in corpore suo pugnam hanc Carnis contra Spiritum, sed erigat se his verbis Pauli: 'Caro concupiscit adversus spiritum' etc., Item: 'Haec sibi invicem adversantur, ut non, quae volueritis, illa faciatis,' His enim sententiis consolatur tentatos, Quasi dicat: Impossible est, ut per omnia sequamini ducem Spiritum sine

ullo sensu aut impedimento Carnis. Imo caro obstabit, et ita obstabit, ut non possitis facere, quae libenter velletis. Hic satis est, ut Carni resistatis, ne concupiscentiam eius perficiatis, hoc est, ut Spiritum sequentes non Carnem, quae facile impacientia frangitur, cupit vindictam, murmurat, odit, mordet, etc. Itaque cum aliquis sentit hanc carnis pugnam, non ideo abiiciat animum, sed resistat Spiritu et dicat: Ego sum peccator et peccatum sentio, quia carne nondum exutus sum, in qua tantisper haeret peccatum, donec vivit, Sed Spiritui, non carni obsequar, Hoc est, apprehendam fide et spe Christum ac ipsius verbo me erigam atque hoc modo erectus concupiscentiam carnis non perficiam." WA 40/2:91, 16-30.

9. *Lectures on Galatians* (1535), *LW* 27:81. "Et hic locus . . . gravissimam consolationem nobis affert, quia admonet, quod sine concupiscentia et tentationibus carnis, imo etiam sine peccatis vivere non possimus. Admonet igitur nos, ne faciamus, ut quidam, de quibus Gerson scribit, qui eo nitebantur, ut prorsus nihil tentationum et peccatorum sentirent, hoc est, ut plane saxa essent. Talem imaginationem habuerunt Sophistae et Monachi de Sanctis, quasi fuerint meri stipites et trunci et plane caruerint omnibus affectibus. Certe Maria sensit maximum dolorem animi amisso filio, Luc. 2. Conqueritur David passim in Psalmis, se immodica tristicia propter magnitudinem tentationum et peccatorum suorum concepta pene absorberi. Conqueritur et Paulus se 'foris pugnas, intus pavores' sentire, Se 'carne servire legi peccati'. Ait se 'solicitum esse pro omnibus Ecclesiis', Et 'Deum misertum esse sui, quod Epaphroditum vicinum morti restituerit vitae, ne dolorem super dolorem haberet'. Itaque Sophistarum Sancti similes sunt Sapientibus Stoicorum." WA 40/2:102, 17-30.

10. *Lectures on Galatians* (1535), *LW* 27:70 (translation modified). "Paulus, cum dicit Carnem concupiscere adversus Spiritum etc., simul commonefacit nos, quod sensuri simus concupiscentiam carnis, hoc est, non solum libidinem, sed superbiam, iram, tristiciam, impacientiam, incredulitatem etc. Verum ita vult nos ista sentire, ne illis consentiamus aut ea perficiamus, Hoc est, ne illa loquamur et faciamus, ad quae nos solicitat caro, Ut, si etiam nos ad iram commoveat, tamen ita 'irascamur', ut Psal. 4. docet, 'ne peccemus.' Quasi sic velit dicere Paulus: Scio, quod solicitabimini a carne ad iram, invidiam, dubitationem, incredulitatem etc., sed resistite Spiritu, ne peccetis. Si vero deserto duce Spiritu Carnem sequimini, concupiscentiam carnis perficietis et 'moriemini', Rom. 8." WA 40/2:88, 17-26.

11. *Lectures on Galatians* (1535), *LW* 26:189. "Ideo nemo sibi confidat, ut existimet se post acceptam gratiam prorsus purgatum esse a veteribus vitiis. Multa quidem purgantur, praecipue autem istum caput serpentis, hoc est incredulitas et ignorantia Dei, praeciditur et conteritur, sed squamosum corpus et reliquiae peccati manent in nobis. Ideo nemo praesumat accepta iam fide se in totum statim transmutari posse in novum hominem, Verum retinebit aliquid priorum vitiorum etiam in Christianismo. Nondum enim mortui sumus, sed vivimus adhoc in carne, Quae, quia nondum est pura, concupiscit adversus spiritum . . . Quare naturalia vitia ante fidem, manent et post fidem acceptam, nisi quod iam servire coguntur spiritui qui eis dominatur, ne regnent, non tamen sine lucta." WA 40/1:312, 29–313, 21.

12. *Lectures on Galatians* (1535), *LW* 27:80–82; WA 40/2:100, 28–102, 16; WA 40/2:104, 7-17.

13. *Lectures on Galatians* (1535), LW 27:82 (translation modified). "Quod omnes aeque non sunt firmi, sed multae adhuc imbecillitates et offensiones cernuntur in quibusdam, Item quod plerique etiam ruunt in peccata, hoc nihil impedit eorum sanctitatem, modo non ex destinata malicia, sed ex imbecillitate peccent. Nam, ut iam aliquoties dixi, pii sentiunt concupiscentiam carnis, sed repugnant, ne eam perficiant. Item, si etiam ex improvisio prolabantur in peccatum, tamen veniam consequuntur, si rursum fide ad Christum accesserint, qui non vult, ut abigamus, sed quaeramus perditam ovem etc. Absit igitur, ut infirmos in fide aut moribus, si videro eos amare et revereri verbum, coena Dominica uti etc., statim iudicem profanos esse, hos enim Deus assumpsit et reputat eos iustos per remissionem peccatorum. Huic 'stant et cadunt.'" WA 40/2:104, 7-17.

Chapter 9: The Sighing of the Spirit

1. *Lectures on Galatians* (1535), *LW* 26:382; WA 40/1:582, 22-27.

2. *Lectures on Galatians* (1535), *LW* 26:381, 383; WA 40/1:580, 25-27; WA 40/1:583, 16-17.

3. *Lectures on Galatians* (1535), *LW* 26:382; WA 40/1:581, 9-31.

4. *Lectures on Galatians* (1535), *LW* 26:382. "Verbum solum habemus, quo apprehenso in illa lucta respiramus paululum ac ingemiscimus, huncque nostrum gemitum aliquo modo sentimus, clamorem vero non audimus." WA 40/1:582, 24-26.

5. *Lectures on Galatians* (1535), *LW* 26:382; WA 40/1:582, 29-33.

6. *Lectures on Galatians* (1535), *LW* 26:382–83 (translation modified). "Apud nos vero est omnino contrarius sensus. Non videtur iste exiguus noster gemitus ita penetrare nubes, quod solus audiatur in coelo a Deo et Angelis, Imo putamus, praesertim durante tentatione, diabolum horribiliter contra nos rugire, coelum mugire, terram tremere, omnia collapsura esse, omnes creaturas minari malum, infernum aperiri ac velle nos deglutire. Hic sensus est in corde nostro, has horribiles voces, hanc terrificam faciem nos audimus et videmus. Atque hoc est, quod Paul. 2. Corin. 12. dicit: 'Potentiam Christi in infirmitate nostra perfici.' Est enim Christus tum vere omnipotens, tum vere regnat ac triumphat in nobis, quando nos, ut sic dicam, sumus ita omniinfirmi, ut vix gemitum aedere possimus. Verum Paulus dicit eum gemitum in auribus Dei esse fortissimum clamorem, qui totum coelum ac terram repleat." WA 40/1:583, 8-19.

7. *Lectures on Galatians* (1535), *LW* 26:383. "Sic Christus quoque Luce 18 in parabola de iniquo Iudice vocat istum gemitum cordis pii clamorem, et talem clamorem, qui indesinenter die ac nocte clamet ad Deum, cum inquit: 'Audite, quid Iudex iniquus dicat. Num igitur Deus non faceret vindictam electorum suorum clamantium ad se die ac nocte et patientiam haberet super illis? Dico vobis, cito faciet vindictam illorum.' Nos hodie in tanta persecutione et contradictione Papae, tyrannorum ac phanaticorum spirituum, qui impugnant nos a dextris et sinistris, nihil possumus quam edere tales gemitus, ac isti fuerunt bombardae ac instrumenta nostra bellica, quibus dissipavimus tot annis consilia adversariorum, quibus demoliri coepimus Antichristi regnum." WA 40/1:583, 20-29.

8. *Lectures on Galatians* (1535), *LW* 26:383. "Sic in Exodo dicit Dominus Mosi ad mare rubrum: 'Quid clamas ad me?' Moses nihil minus faciebat, sed erat in summis angustiis. Ideo tremebat ac paene desperabat. Incredulitas videbatur regnare in eo, non fides. Erat enim Israel ita montibus, exercitu Aegyptiorum ac mari conclusus, ut nusquam posset aufugere. Hic Moses ne mutire quidem audebat, quomodo igitur clamavit? Itaque non debemus iudicare secundum sensum cordis nostri, sed secundum verbum Dei, quod docet Spiritum sanctum ideo donari afflictis, conterritis, desperabundis etc., ut eos erigat ac consoletur, ne in tentationibus et omnibus malis succumbant, sed ea vincant, non tamen sine maximis pavoribus et laboribus." WA 40/1:583, 20-29.

9. *Lectures on Galatians* (1535), *LW* 26:384. "In his autem proprie exercet (sc. Spiritus sanctus) opus suum, qui vehementer conterriti sunt

et appropinquaverunt, ut Psalm. ait, usque ad 'portas mortis,' Ut de Mose iam dixi, qui videbat praesentissimam mortem in aquis et quoquo vertebat vultum. Fuit igitur in summa angustia et desperatione proculque dubio sensit in corde fortissimum clamorem Diaboli contra se, dicentis: Iste totus populus hodie peribit, nusquam enim potest elabi. Huius maximi mali tu solus eris author, quia eduxisti eum ex Aegypto. Accessit denique clamor populi, qui dixit: 'An non erant sepulchra in Aegypto? Tu ideo eduxisti nos, ut hic moreremur in deserto. An non melius fuisset servire Aegyptiis quam hic misere nos mori in deserto?' Ibi Spiritus sanctus non fuit speculative in Mose, sed re vera, qui pro ipso interpellavit gemitu inenarrabile, ut suspiraret Moses ad Deum et diceret: Domine, tuo iussu eduxi populum, Fer igitur opem. Hunc gemitum vocat 'clamorem.'" WA 40/1:584, 27–585, 17.

Chapter 10: Realistic Symbolism and the Union with Christ

1. *Lectures on Galatians* (1535), *LW* 26:391; WA 40/1:596, 18-20.

2. *Lectures on Galatians* (1535), *LW* 26:385; WA 40/1:586, 18-26.

3. *Lectures on Galatians* (1535), *LW* 26:375; cf. also ibid., 391–92; WA 40/1:572, 16-21; cf. also ibid., 596, 20-30.

4. *Lectures on Galatians* (1535), *LW* 26:449. "Appellat etiam Ecclesiam sterilem, quia filii ipsius non lege, operibus, non ullis conatibus aut viribus humanis, sed in Spiritu sancto per verbum fidei generantur. Ibi mera nascentia est, nulla operatio. Contra foecundi laborant et exercent se nimium parturiendo ibique mera operatio est, nulla nativitas." WA 40/1:674, 21-25.

5. *Lectures on Galatians* (1535), *LW* 26:392. "Nam qui filius est, illum et haeredem esse oportet. Hoc ipso enim, quod nascitur, meretur esse haeres. Nullum opus, nullum meritum affert ei haereditatem, sed sola nativitas. Atque ita mere passive, non active contingit ei haereditas. hoc est, ipsum nasci, non gignere, non laborare, non curare etc. facit eum haeredem. Nihil enim facit ad hoc, ut nascatur, sed tantum patitur. Itaque passive, non active pervenimus ad ista aeterna bona, remissionem peccatorum, iustitiam, resurrectionis gloriam et ad vitam aeternam. Nihil prorsus hic intercedit, sola fides apprehendit oblatam promissionem. Sicut ergo filius in politia tantum nascendo fit haeres, Sic hic sola fides efficit filios Dei, natos ex verbo, quod est uterus divinus, in quo concipimur, gestamur, nascimur, educamur etc. Hac ergo nativitate, hac patientia seu passione, qua fimus Christiani, fimus etiam filii et haeredes. Existentes

autem haeredes liberi sumus a morte, diabolo etc. et habemus iustitiam et vitam aeternam." WA 40/1:597, 15-28.

6. *Lectures on Galatians* (1535), *LW* 26:441–42. "Quare sicut Isaac haereditatem patris habet solum ex promissione et nativitate, sine Lege et operibus. Ita nos per Evangelium nascimur heredes ex Sara libera, id est, Ecclesia. Ea enim docet, fovet, gestat nos in utero, gremio et ulnis, fingit et perficit nos ad formam Christi, donec crescamus in virum perfectum etc. Ita omnia fiunt per ministerium verbi." WA 40/1:665, 13-17.

7. *Lectures on Galatians* (1535), *LW* 26:441. "Quare Sara seu Hierusalem, mater nostra libera, est ipsa Ecclesia, Christi sponsa, ex qua generamur omnes. Generat autem ipsa liberos sine intermissione usque ad finem mundi, dum exercet ministerium verbi, hoc est, dum docet et propagat Evangelium, hoc enim generare est." WA 40/1:664, 18-21.

8. [*LW*: "the form of the mind"—Ed.]

9. *Lectures on Galatians* (1535), *LW* 26:430 (translation modified). "'Quos iterum parturio': Allegoria est. Apostoli (ut etiam praeceptores, suo tamen modo) funguntur vice parentum; ut enim hi formam corporis, ita illi formam animi generant. Est autem forma Christiani animi fides seu fiducia cordis, quae apprehendit Christum, illi soli adhaeret et nulli praeterea rei. Cor tali fiducia praeditum habet veram formam Christi. Ea autem paratur ministerio verbi . . . Verbum enim procedit ex ore Apostoli et pertingit ad cor audientis; ibi Spiritus sanctus adest et imprimit in cor illud verbum, ut sonat. Hoc modo omnis Doctor pius est parens, qui per ministerium verbi generat et format veram figuram Christiani animi." WA 40/1:649, 19-30.

Chapter 11: The Present Christ and the Objective Basis for Holiness

1. See Tuomo Mannermaa, *Kaksi Rakkautta: Johdatus Lutherin Uskonmaailmaan* [Two kinds of love: Introduction to Luther's world of faith] (Juva, 1983).

2. *Lectures on Galatians* (1535), *LW* 26:431; WA 40/1:650, 3-10.

3. "Imago Christi, dei: ita sentire, affici, velle, intelligere, cogitare sicut Christus vel ipsum Christum. Est autem ista voluntas, spiritus Christi, quod mortuus pro peccatis nostris ad obedientam patris, hoc credere est habere imaginem quam Christus. Das ist 'novus homo, qui generatur' etc." WA 40/1:650, 5-9.

4. *Lectures on Galatians* (1535), *LW* 26:431; WA 40/1:650, 30-31 (published text).

5. *Lectures on Galatians* (1535), *LW* 27:83. "Admiratur mundus sanctitatem Benedicti, Gregorii, Bernhardi, Francisci et similium, quia audit eos magnifica in speciem et insolita quaedam opera fecisse. Certe fuerunt etiam Sancti Ambrosius, Augustinus et alii, qui tam asperam et horridam vitam non egerunt ut illi, sed conversati sunt inter homines, ederunt cibos communes, biberunt vinum et vestitu eleganti ac decenti usi sunt et fere nullum discrimen fuit, quod ad communem vitae consuetudinem attinet, inter ipsos et alios honestos viros, et tamen longe praeferendi sunt illis superioribus. Hi enim sine ulla superstitione docuerunt fidem Christi pure, Haereticis restiterunt et Ecclesiam ab innumeris erroribus repurgaverunt. Iucundissima fuit multis eorum familiaritas, et praesertim tristibus et afflictis (non enim abduxerunt se a conversatione hominum, sed officium suum administraverunt in frequenti turba), quos verbo erexerunt et consolati sunt. Contra illi non solum contra fidem multa docuerunt, sed etiam multarum superstitionum, errorum et impiorum cultuum autores fuerunt. Ideo nisi in agone mortis Christum apprehenderunt et sola ipsius morte et victoria confisi sunt, nihil plane profuit eis rigida vita." WA 40/2:104, 30–105, 22.

6. *Lectures on Galatians* (1535), *LW* 27:84; WA 40/2:105, 23–106, 18.

7. *Lectures on Galatians* (1535), *LW* 27:84; WA 40/2:106, 21-23.

8. *Lectures on Galatians* (1535), *LW* 27:85; WA 40/2:106, 29-30.

9. *In epistolam S. Pauli ad Galatas Commentarius ex praelectione D. Martini Luther collectus* (1535), WA 40/1:228, 33–229, 15. "Christ is the object of faith, or rather not the object but, so to speak, the One who is present in the faith itself." *Lectures on Galatians* (1535), *LW* 26:129.

Select Bibliography

I. Works of Tuomo Mannermaa

1968

Kaikki uudeksi. Uppsalassa 4.-20. heinäkuuta 1968 pidettävän Kirkkojen maailmanneuvoston neljännen yleiskokouksen valmistelukirjanen. [A preparation document of the 4th meeting of the WCC.] Tuomo Mannermaa. Suomen ekumeenisen neuvoston julkaisuja XIII. Helsinki.

1970

Lumen fidei et obiectium fidei adventicium. Uskontiedon spontaanisuus ja reseptiivisyys Karl Rahnerin varhaisessa ajattelussa. [Spontaneity and receptivity in Karl Rahner's early thought.] Missiologian ja ekumeniikan seuran julkaisuja (MESJ) 19. Kuopio.

1973

(with Simo Kiviranta). "Genesis und Struktur. Das Problem der Einheitlichkeit des Leuenberger Konkordienentwurfs." *Von der wahren Einheit der Kirche. Lutherische Stimmen zum Leuenberger Konkordienentwurf.* Ed. Ulrich Asendorf and Friedrich Wilhelm Künneth. Berlin.

1976

"Katholizität der Kirche in den evangelish-lutherischen Bekenntnisscriften. Kirche – Sakrament – Amt." *Deutschskandinavische Theologentagung von 25. – 28. August in Ratzeburg.* Ed. Ulrich Asendorf and J. Heubach. Hamburg, 130–134.

1977

"Kenellä on valta kirkossa Lutherin mukaan?" [Who has the power in the church according to Luther?] *Iustificatio impii. Jumalattoman vanhurskauttaminen.* Juhlakirja Lauri Haikolan täyttäessä 60 vuotta 9.2. 1977. (Festschrift for Lauri Haikola.) Jussi Talasniemi. STKSJ 103. Helsinki, 1977, 161–165.

Kristillisen opin vaiheet. Dogmihistorian peruskurssi. [The development of Christian doctrine. The foundations of the history of the dogma.] Helsinki, 1975.

"Raamatullisuus kirkossa." [<**KS: Better Translation?**>Biblical in church.] *Mitä on raamatullisuus.* Pieksämäki, 12–18.

1978

Preussista Leuenbergiin. Leuenbergin konkordian teologinen methodi. [From Preuss to Leuenberg. The theological method of the Leuenberg concord.] MESJ 29. Vammala.

1979

In ipsa fide Christus adest. Luterilaisen ja ortodoksisen kristinuskonkäsityksen leikkauspiste. MESJ 30. Helsinki. In German: "In ipsa fide Christus adest. Der Schnittpunkt zwischen lutherischer und orthodoxer Theologie," in Tuomo Mannermaa, *Der im Glauben gegenwärtige Christus. Rechtfertigung und Vergottung. Zum ökumenischen Dialog.* Arbeiten zur Geschichte und Theologie des Luthertums. Neue Folge, Band 8; Hannover: Lutherisches Verlagshaus, 1989, 11–93.

Kontrapunkteja. Teologisia tutkimuksia ajankohtaisista teemoista. [Counterpoints. Theological studies on current themes.] STKSJ 122. Vammala, 1979.

1981

"Puun täytyy kantaa hedelmää." [The tree must bear fruit.] *Luterilainen usko tänään. Augsbugin tunnustuksen selityksiä.* [Lutheran faith today. Interpretations of the Augsburg Confession.] Ed. Simo Kiviranta. Vaasa 1981, 46–49.

1982

Von Preussen nach Leuenberg. Hintergrund und Entwicklung der theologischen Methode der Leuenberger Konkordie. Arbeiten zur Geschichte und Theologie des Luthertums. Neue Folge, Band 1. Hamburg, 1982.

1983

Kaksi rakkautta. Johdatus Lutherin uskonmaailmaan. [Two kinds of love. Introduction to Luther's world of faith.] Juva.

"Theosis und das Böse bei Luther." *Makarios-Symposium über das Böse.* Vorträge der Finnische-deutschen Theologentagung in Goslar 1980. Ed. Werner Strothmann. Wiesbaden, 170–79.

1984

"Das Verhältnis von Glaube und Liebe in der Theologie Luthers." *Luther in Finnland.* Ed. Miikka Ruokanen. Schriften der Luther-Agricola-Gesellschaft A 23. Vammala, 99–110.

"Laupiaan samarialaisen teologia." [Theology of the samaritan.] *Diakonian vuosikirja* 1984. [The yearbook of diakonia 1984]. Helsinki, 19–26.

"Rakkaus Jumalaan Lutherin teologiassa." [Love of God in Luther's theology.] *Elevatis Oculis. Studia mystica in honorem Seppo A. Teinonen.* Ed. Pauli Annala. MESJ 42. Vammala, 1984, 144–54.

1987

"Grundlagenforschung der Theologie Martin Luthers und die Ökumene." *Thesaurus Lutheri,* 17–35.

Mannermaa, Tuomo. 1989. *Der im Glauben gegenwärtige Christus. Rechtfertigung und Vergottung.* Arbeiten zur Geschichte und Theologie des Luthertums. Neue Folge, Band 8, Hannover.

1990

"Theosis als Thema der finnischen Lutherforschung." *Luther und Theosis,* 11–26.

1991

"Diakonian teologiaa vanhasta kirkosta reformaation." [Theology of diakonia from the early church to the Reformation.] *Hoivatkaa toinen toistanne. Diakonian teologian käsikirja.* [Care for each other: The handbook of diaconal theology.] Ed. Kerttu Inkala. Pieksämäki, 39–47.

"Kirkon uudistus, rakkaus ja luterilainen perintö." [Renewal of the church, love, and the Lutheran tradition.] *Purjeena perinne. Juhlakirja Arkkipiispa John Vikströmin täyttäessä 60 vuotta.* [Sailing with the tradition. Festschrift to honor Archbishop John Vikström.] Turun arkkihiippakunnan vuosikirja 41. Turku, 74–79.

"Liebe VI. Reformation und Orthodoxie." *Theologische Realenzyklopädie (TRE).* Band 21. Salzweg-Passau, 152–56.

"Rukouksen teologia – keskeneräinen tehtävä akatemian ja kirkon välimaastossa." [Theology of prayer – An unfinished task in the space between church and academy.] *Academia et ecclesia. Studia in honorem Fredric Cleve.* Ed. Hans-Olof Kvist. Åbo, 140–45.

1993

"Hat Luther eine trinitarische Ontologie?" *Luther und Ontologie. Das Sein Christi im Glauben als strukturierendes Prinzip der Theologie Luthers.* Referate der Fachtagung des Instituts für Systematische Theologie der Universitet Helsinki in Zusammenarbeit mit der Luther-Akademie Ratzeburg in Helsinki 1.-5.4.1992. Ed. Anja Ghiselli, Kari Kopperi, Rainer Vinke. Schriften der Luther-Agricola-Gesellschaft A 31. Veröffentlichungen der Luther-Akademie Ratzeburg. Band 21. Vammala, 9–27.

Nordisk Forum för studiet av Luther och luthersk teologi 1. Referate des ersten Forums für das Studium von Luther und lutherischer Theologie in Helsinki 21.-24.11.1991. Ed. Tuomo Mannermaa, Petri Järveläinen, Kari Kopperi. Schriften der Luther Agricola-Gesellschaft A 28. Helsinki.

"Theologische Ontologie bei Luther?" *Nordisk Forum för studiet av Luther och luthersk teologi* 1 (see above), 37–53.

1994

"Hat Luther eine trinitarische Ontologie?" *Luther und die trinitarische Tradition: ökumenische und philosophische Perspektiven.* Ed. Joachim Heubach. Veröffentlichungen der Luther-Akademie Ratzeburg. Band 23. Erlangen. 43–60.

1995

"Freiheit als Liebe: Einführung in das Thema." *Freiheit als Liebe bei Martin Luther.* 8th International Congress for Luther Research in St. Paul, Minnesota 1993: Seminar 1 Referate/Papers. Frankfurt am Main. Ed. Klaus Schwarzwäller und Dennis Bielfeldt, 9–18.

"Grund der Freiheit in der Theologie Martin Luthers. "*Kirche in der Schule Luthers: Festschrift für D. Joachim Heubach.* Martin-Luther-Verlag, Erlangen, 79–89.

Kaksi rakkautta. Johdatus Lutherin uskonmaailmaan. [Two kinds of love. Introduction to Luther's world of faith.] 2nd ed. STKSJ 194. Helsinki.

Pieni kirja Jumalasta. [A small book on God.] Jyväskylä.

"Vorwort." In *Freiheit als Liebe bei Martin Luther* (see above).

1996

"Die lutherische Theologie und die Theologie der Liebe." *In der Wahrheit bleiben: Dogma - Schriftauslegung - Kirche. Festschrift für Reinhard Slenczka.* Ed. Manfred Seitz und Karsten Lehmkühler. Göttingen: Vandenhoeck, 111–19.

"Vapauden perusta Lutherin teologiassa." (The foundation of freedom in Luther's theology.) *Jumalan kansan tie. Simo Kivirannan 60-vuotisjuhlakirja.* [The road of God's people.

Festschrift for Simo Kiviranta.] Ed. Reijo Arkkila, Erkki Koskenniemi, Seppo Suokunnas. Jyväskylä, 33–36.

"Über die Unmöglichkeit, gegen Texte Luthers zu systematisieren: Antwort an Gunther Wenz." *Unio*, 381–91.

1997

"Participation and Love in the Theology of Martin Luther." *Philosophical Studies in Religion, Metaphysics and Ethics. Essays in Honor of Heikki Kirjavainen.* Ed. Timo Koistinen and Tommi Lehtonen. Schriften der Luther-Agricola Gesellschaft 38. Helsinki, 303–11.

1998

"Justification and Theosis in Lutheran-Orthodox Perspective." *Union With Christ: The New Finnish Interpretation of Luther.* Ed. Carl E. Braaten and Robert W. Jenson. Grand Rapids: Eerdmans, 25–41.

"Why Is Luther So Fascinating? Modern Finnish Luther Research." *Union with Christ*, 1–20.

1999

"Zur Kritik der jüngeren finnischen Lutherforschung." *Informationes theologiae Europeae. Internationales ökumenisches Jahrbuch für Theologie.* Frankfurt, 171–86.

2000

"Doctrine of Justification and Trinitarian Ontology." *Trinity, Time and Church: A Response to the Theology of Robert W. Jenson.* Ed. C. Gunton. Grand Rapids: Eerdmans, 139–45.

II. Finnish Luther Research

Multi-authored Volumes (in chronological order)

Thesaurus Lutheri. 1987. Auf der Suche nach neuen Paradigmen der Luther-Forschung. Ed. Tuomo Mannermaa, Anja Ghiselli und Simo Peura. Veröffentlichungen der Finnischen Theologischen

Literaturgesellschaft 153. Schriften der Luther-Agricola-Gesellschaft A 24. Helsinki.

Luther und Theosis. 1990. Vergöttlichung als Thema der abendländischen Theologie. Ed. Simo Peura und Antti Raunio. Schriften der Luther-Agricola-Gesellschaft A 25 und Veröffentlichungen der Luther-Akademie Ratzeburg, Band. 15. Helsinki und Erlangen.

Luther und Ontologie. 1993. Das Sein Christi im Glauben als strukturierendes Prinzip der Theologie Luthers. Ed. Anja Ghiselli, Kari Kopperi, Reiner Vinke. Schriften der Luther-Agricola-Gesellschaft 31. Veröffentlichungen der Luther-Akademie Ratzeburg. Helsinki und Erlangen.

Nordiskt Forum för Studiet av Luther och luthersk teologi 1. 1993. Ed. Tuomo Mannermaa, Petri Järveläinen, Kari Kopperi. Referate des ersten Forums für das Studium von Luther und lutherischer Theologie. Schriften der Luther-Agricola-Gesellschaft 28. Helsinki.

Luther und die trinitarische Tradition. 1994. Ökumenische und trinitarische Perspektiven. Ed. Joachim Heubach. Veröffentlichungen der Luther-Akademie Ratzeburg 23. Martin-Luther-Verlag, Erlangen.

Unio. 1996. Gott und Mensch in der nachreformatorischen Theologie. Ed. Matti Repo und Rainer Vinke. Veröffentlichungen der Finnischen Theologischen Literaturgesellschaft 200. Schriften der Luther-Agricola Gesellschaft 35. Helsinki.

Widerspruch. 1996. Luthers Auseinandersetzung mit Erasmus von Rotterdam. Nordiskt Forum 2. Ed. Kari Kopperi. Schriften der Luther-Agricola-Gesellschaft 37. Helsinki.

Der Heilige Geist. 1996. Ökumenische und reformatorische Untersuchungen. Ed. Joachim Heubach. Veröffentlichungen der Luther-Akademie Ratzeburg 25. Martin-Luther-Verlag, Erlangen.

Caritas Dei. 1997. Beiträge zum Verständnis Luthers und der gegenwärtigen Ökumene. Festschrift für Tuomo Mannermaa. Ed. Oswald Bayer, Robert Jenson, Simo Knuuttila. Schriften der Luther-Agricola-Gesellschaft 39. Helsinki.

Union With Christ: The New Finnish Interpretation of Luther. 1998. Ed. Carl E. Braaten and Robert W. Jenson. Grand Rapids: Eerdmans.

Articles in Multi-author Volumes

Huovinen, Eero. 1987. "Fides infantium - fides infusa? Ein Beitrag zum Verständnis des Kinderglaubens bei Luther." *Thesaurus Lutheri*, 155–70.

Huovinen, Eero. 1990. "Opus operatum. Ist Luthers Verständnis von der Effektivität des Sakraments richtig verstanden?" *Luther und Theosis*, 187–214.

Huovinen, Eero. 1997. "Der infusio-Gedanke als Problem der Lutherforschung." *Caritas Dei*, 192–204.

Juntunen, Sammeli. 1998. "Luther and Metaphysics: What Is the Structure of Being according to Luther?" *Union with Christ*, 129–60.

Kirjavainen, Heikki. 1987. "Die Spezifierung der Glaubensgegenstände bei Luther im Licht der Spätmittelalterlichen Semantik." *Thesaurus Lutheri*, 237–57.

Knuuttila, Simo. 1987. "Remarks on Late Medieval and Early Modern Theories about Eternal Truths." *Thesaurus Lutheri*, 53–62.

Knuuttila, Simo, and Risto Saarinen. 1997. "Innertrinitarische Theologie in der Scholastik und bei Luther." *Caritas Dei*, 243–64.

Kopperi, Kari. 1993. "Luthers theologische Zielsetzung in den philosophischen Thesen der Heidelberger Disputation." *Nordiskt Forum* 1, 67–103.

Martikainen, Eeva. 1990. "Die Lehre und die Gegenwart Gottes in der Theologie Luthers." *Luther und theosis*, 215–32.

Martikainen, Eeva. 1997. "Der Begriff 'Gott' in De servo arbitrio." *Widerspruch*, 26–45.

Martikainen, Eeva. 1987. "Der Doctrina-Begriff in Luthers Theologie." *Thesaurus Lutheri*, 205–19.

Peura, Simo. 1987. "Der Vergöttlichungsgedanke in Luthers Theologie 1517–1519." *Thesaurus Lutheri*, 171–84.

Peura, Simo. 1990. "Die Teilhabe an Christus bei Luther." *Luther und theosis*, 121–62.

Peura, Simo. 1993. "Wort, Sakrament und Sein Gottes." *Luther und Ontologie*, 35–69.

Peura, Simo. 1994. "Das Sich-Geben Gottes: Korreferat zu Ulrich Asendorf. Die Trinitätslehre als integrales Problem der Theologie Martin Luthers." *Luther und die trinitarische Tradition*, 131–46.

Peura, Simo. 1996a. "Die Kirche als geistliche communio bei Luther." *Der Heilige Geist*, 131–56.

Peura, Simo. 1996b. "Gott und Mensch in der Unio: Die Unterschiede im Rechtfertigungsverständnis bei Osiander und Luther." *Unio*, 33–61.

Peura, Simo. 1997. "Christus als Gunst und Gabe." *Caritas Dei*, 340–63.

Peura, Simo. 1998a. "Christ as Favor and Gift: The Challenge of Luther's Understanding of Justification." *Union with Christ*, 42–69.

Peura, Simo. 1998b. "What God Gives Man Receives: Luther on Salvation." *Union with Christ*, 76–95.

Raunio, Antti. 1987. "Die 'Goldene Regel' als theologisches Prinzip beim jungen Luther." *Thesaurus Lutheri*, 309–27.

Raunio, Antti. 1996. "Die Gegenwart des Geistes im Christen bei Luther." *Der Heilige Geist*, 89–104.

Raunio, Antti.1990. "Die Goldene Regel als Gesetz der göttlichen Natur." *Luther und theosis*, 163–86.

Ruokanen, Miikka. 1987. "Does Luther Have a Theory of Biblical Inspiration?" *Thesaurus Lutheri*, 259–78.

Single-author Works

Forsberg, Juhani. 1984. *Das Abrahambild in der Theologie Luthers: Pater fidei sanctissimus.* Veröffentlichungen des Institut für europäische Geschichte Mainz, Band. 117. Frans Steiner Verlag. Wiesbaden.

Huovinen, Eero. 1997a. *Fides infantium. Martin Luthers Lehre vom Kinderglauben.* Veröffentlichungen des Institut für Europäische Geschichte Mainz, Band. 159. Philipp von Zabern, Mainz.

Huovinen, Eero. 1997b. "Martin Luthers Lehre vom Kinderglauben: fides infantium als reale Gabe Gottes und reale Teilhabe an Gott." *Das Sakrament der heiligen Taufe.* Ed. J. Heubach. Luther-Akademie Ratzeburg, Martin-Luther-Verlag, Erlangen 1997, 41–61.

Juntunen, Sammeli. 1996. *Der Begriff des Nichts bei Luther in den Jahren von 1510 bis 1523.* Schriften der Luther-Agricola Gesellschaft 36. Helsinki.

Juntunen, Sammeli. 1999. "Der Begriff des Nichts bei Luther." Mensch—Gott—Menschwerdung. Texte aus der VELKD. Hannover, 79–99.

Kirjavainen, Heikki. 1986. "Die Paradoxie des Simul-Prinzips." *Neue Zeitschrift für Systematische Theologie und Religionsphilosophie* 28:29–50.

Knuuttila, Simo. 1998. "Luther's View of Logic and the Revelation." *Medioevo* 24:219–34.

Knuuttila, Simo, and Risto Saarinen. 1999. "Luther's Trinitarian Theology and Its Medieval Background." *Studia theologica* 53:3–12.

Kopperi, Kari. 1997. *Paradoksien teologia. Lutherin disputaatio Heidelbergissä 1518.* [Theology of paradox. Luther's Heidelberg Disputation in 1518.] STKS:n julkaisuja 208. (diss.) Helsinki.

Martikainen, Eeva. 1992. *Doctrina. Studien zu Luthers Begriff der Lehre.* Luther-Agricola Society, Helsinki.

Martikainen, Eeva. 1988. "Lutherforschung in Finnland seit 1934." *Theologische Rundschau* 53.

Peura, Simo. 1993a. "Christus praesentissmus: The Issue of Luther's Thought in the Lutheran-Orthodox Dialogue." *Pro Ecclesia* 2:364–71.

Peura, Simo. 1993b. "Die Vergöttlichung des Menschen als Sein in Gott." *Luther-Jahrbuch* 60, 39–71.

Peura, Simo. 1994. *Mehr als ein Mensch? Die Vergöttlichung als Thema der Theologie Martin Luthers von 1513 bis 1519.* Veröffentlichungen des Institut für Europäische Geschichte Mainz. Philipp von Zabern, Mainz.

Peura, Simo. 1998. "In memoriam Lennart Pinomaa." *Luther-Jahrbuch* 65, 11–14.

Peura, Simo. 1999. "Luthers Verständnis der Rechtefertigung: forensisch oder effektiv?" *Recent Research on Martin Luther,* Evangelical Theological Faculty, Bratislava 1999, 34–57.

Raunio, Antti. 1993. *Summe des christlichen Lebens. Die "Goldene Regel" als Gesetz der Liebe in der Theologie Martin Luthers von 1510 bis 1527.* Helsingin yliopiston systemaattisen teologian laitoksen julkaisuja XIII. Helsinki. Diss.

Raunio, Antti. 1996. "The Golden Rule as the Summary of the Sermon on the Mount in the Reformed and Lutheran Traditions." *Towards a Renewed Dialogue: The First and Second Reformations.* Ed. Milan Opocensky. Studies from the World Alliance of Reformed Churches 30. Geneva, 122–42.

Raunio, Antti. 1999a. "Natural Law and Faith: The Foundations of Ethics in Luther's Theology." *Recent Research on Martin Luther.* Evangelical Theological Faculty, Bratislava, 9–33.

Raunio, Antti. 1999b. "The Church as Diaconal Communion: Some Signposts for the Renewal of the Church." *Recent Research on Martin Luther.* Evangelical Theological Faculty, Bratislava, 73–84.

Raunio, Antti. 2000. "Glaube und Liebe in der Theologie Martin Luthers in ihrer Bedeutung für die diakonische Praxis." *Diakonie an der Schwelle zum neuen Jahrtausend.* Heidelberg, 172–87.

Ruokanen, Miikka. 1985. *Doctrina divinitus inspirata. Martin Luther's position in the ecumenical problem of biblical inspiration.* Publications of Luther-Agricola Society B 14. Helsinki.

Saarinen, Risto. 1988. "Metapher und biblische Redefiguren als Elemente der Sprachphilosophie Luthers." *Neue Zeitschrift für systematische Theologie und Religionsphilosophie* 30:18–39.

Saarinen, Risto. 1989. *Gottes Wirken auf uns. Die transzendentale Deutung des Gegenwart-Christi-Motivs in der Lutherforschung.* Veröffentlichungen des Instituts für Europäische Geschichte Mainz, Band. 137. Frans Steiner, Wiesbaden.

Saarinen, Risto. 1990. "The Word of God in Luther's Theology." *Lutheran Quarterly,* n.s., 4:31–44.

Saarinen, Risto. 1994. "The Presence of God in Luther's Theology." *Lutheran Quarterly,* n.s., 8:3–14.

Työrinoja, Reijo. 1986. "Proprietas Verbi." *Faith, Will and Grammar.* Ed. H. Kirjavainen. Publications of Luther-Agricola Society B 15. Helsinki, 140–78.

Selected Luther Research Related Websites

http://www.helsinki.fi/~risaarin/luther.html
http://luther.chadwyck.co.uk
http://gallica.bnf.fr
http://staupitz.luthersem.edu
http://www.luthersem.edu/library
http://www.fordham.edu/halsall/mod/modsbook1.html#Luther
http://www.luther.de
http://www.luther-gesellschaft.com
http://www.wittenberg.de
http://www-db.helsinki.fi/julki/

Index

CPSIA information can be obtained at www.ICGtesting.com
Printed in the USA
LVOW05s1351200314

378122LV00007B/102/A